MEDITERRANEAN DIET MASTERY

A Newbie's Guide to Mediterranean Diet Meal Prep.

Quick, Healthy, and Delicious Recipes

You'll Want to Make All the Time

Ivy Starling

TABLE OF CONTENTS

INTRODUCTION 1

    Mediterranean Diet Meal Prep Tips and Tricks.................................. 4

    Key Rules for Shopping on a Mediterranean Diet Meal Prep 5

CHAPTER 1 BREAKFAST RECIPES.. 7

    Muffin-Tin Spanakopita Omelets 9

    Homemade Plain Yogurt 11

    Fig & Ricotta Toast 12

    Cherry-Walnut Overnight Oats.. 13

    Baked Omelet Toast 14

    Shakshuka 16

    Chickpea Toast 18

    Breakfast Quinoa.. 19

    Chicken Meal Prep... 21

    Baked Cod 23

    Greek Yogurt Parfait... 24

    Vegetable Frittata 25

    Greek Spinach and Feta Muffins 27

    Avocado Toast 29

    Greek Yogurt Pancakes... 30

    Mediterranean Egg Wraps 32

    Tofu Scramble with Spinach and Mushrooms................................. 33

    Breakfast BurritoGreek Omelette 35

    Breakfast Quiche 36

CHAPTER 2 LUNCH RECIPES 37

    Greek Salad with Grilled Chicken 39

    Quinoa Salad 41

    Lemon Herb Salmon with Roasted Vegetables................................ 43

    Chickpea and Vegetable Stew 45

Grilled Vegetable Wraps with Hummus 47

Greek Lemon Chicken Skewers with Tzatziki Sauce 48

Mediterranean Couscous Salad 50

Falafel with Tahini Sauce 52

Caprese Salad with Balsamic Glaze 54

Greek Lentil Soup 55

Pasta Salad with Sun-Dried Tomatoes and Olives 56

Shrimp and Feta Orzo Salad 57

Stuffed Bell Peppers with Quinoa and Feta 58

Mediterranean Chickpea Salad 60

Grilled Eggplant and Halloumi Sandwich 61

Lemon Garlic Shrimp with Orzo 62

Tomato and Mozzarella Salad with Basil Pesto 63

Greek Spinach and Feta Pie 64

Mediterranean Stuffed Zucchini Boats 66

Grilled Lamb Kebabs with Yogurt Sauce 68

CHAPTER 3 DINNER RECIPES 69

Greek Lemon Chicken with Roasted Vegetables 71

Mediterranean Stuffed Bell Peppers 73

Baked Salmon with Greek Salad 75

Quinoa Tabbouleh with Grilled Chicken 77

Grilled Shrimp Skewers with Lemon and Herbs 79

Ratatouille with Chickpeas 80

Mediterranean Baked Cod with Tomatoes and Olives 82

Lentil and Vegetable Moussaka 84

Greek Spinach and Feta Stuffed Chicken Breast 86

Mediterranean Grilled Vegetable Wrap 88

Tuscan White Bean Soup with Kale 89

Greek Style Baked Eggplant with Tomato Sauce 91

Lemon Herb Grilled Pork Chops with Mediterranean Couscous 93

Moroccan Spiced Chickpea and Vegetable Tagine 95

Mediterranean Stuffed Zucchini Boats 97

Herb Crusted Baked Cod with Mediterranean Quinoa Pilaf 99

Greek Style Lamb Meatballs with Tzatziki Sauce 101

Mediterranean Quinoa Salad with Roasted Vegetables 103

Shrimp and Vegetable Stir-Fry with Brown Rice 105

Greek Style Baked Falafel with Tzatziki Sauce 107

CHAPTER 4 DESSERT RECIPES 109

Lemon Olive Oil Cake 111

Mediterranean Yogurt Parfait with Fresh Berries and Honey 113

Almond and Orange Blossom Cookies 114

Fig and Walnut Tart 115

Pistachio Baklava 117

Roasted Apricots with Honey and Thyme 119

Greek Yogurt Panna Cotta with Raspberry Sauce 120

Olive Oil and Orange Cake 122

Almond Butter Energy Balls 124

Chocolate Dipped Medjool Dates with Sea Salt 125

Watermelon and Feta Salad with Mint 126

Strawberry Greek Yogurt Frozen Pops 127

Honey Roasted Figs with Greek Yogurt 128

Greek Yogurt Cheesecake with Berry Compote 129

Almond Flour Chocolate Chip Cookies 131

Orange and Almond Semolina Cake 132

Baked Pears with Honey and Cinnamon 134

Greek Yogurt Chocolate Mousse 135

Honey and Lemon Ricotta Tart 136

Walnut and Honey Phyllo Rolls 138

CHAPTER 5 SNACK RECIPES 139

Avocado and Hummus Toast 141

Energy Balls (Variety of Flavors) 142

Roasted Chickpeas (Seasoned with Spices) 143

Guacamole and Veggie Sticks 144

Cucumber Sushi Rolls with Avocado and Carrot..145

Vegan Nachos with Cashew Cheese and Black Beans..................................146

Zucchini Fritters with Tzatziki Sauce 148

Carrot and Beetroot Hummus with Whole Grain Crackers 150

Vegan Caprese Skewers with Cherry Tomatoes, Basil, and Vegan Mozzarella...............152

Roasted Edamame Beans with Sea Salt and Chili Flakes 153

Vegan Buffalo Cauliflower Bites with Ranch Dip 154

Vegan Spring Rolls with Peanut Dipping Sauce 156

Mini Vegan Pizza Bites with Whole Wheat Dough and Veggie Toppings.................158

Baked Kale Chips with Nutritional Yeast 160

Stuffed Mushrooms with Quinoa and Spinach 161

Salsa and Black Bean Stuffed Sweet Peppers 163

Beetroot and Lentil Hummus with Pita Bread......................................164

Cinnamon Apple Chips..165

Zucchini and Corn Fritters with Spicy Chipotle Mayo........................166

Mini Quiches with Tofu and Vegetable Fillings 168

Chocolate Avocado Mousse Cups 170

CONCLUSION..171

INTRODUCTION

The culinary tradition of Mediterranean cuisine is renowned for its rich flavors, vibrant colors, and fresh ingredients. This cuisine has evolved over centuries, showcasing a diverse fusion of culinary influences from the countries surrounding the Mediterranean Sea.

Mediterranean cuisine is not merely a collection of recipes; it is a way of life. The Mediterranean diet, which forms the foundation of this cuisine, has been recognized as one of the healthiest diets in the world. The Mediterranean diet encourages the intake of fruits, vegetables, whole grains, legumes, nuts, and olive oil, while also including moderate portions of fish, poultry, and dairy products. This dietary approach advocates for a well-rounded and balanced consumption of these food groups. The Mediterranean diet is widely known for its effectiveness in promoting overall health and well-being, while also potentially lowering the risk of heart disease, cancer, and other chronic illnesses.

The culinary traditions of the Mediterranean region have been greatly influenced by its diverse geography. Countries like Greece, Italy, Spain, France, Morocco, and Turkey, which are located around the Mediterranean Sea, have their own distinct culinary practices. Despite their differences, they also have shared characteristics that bind them together as part of the broader Mediterranean cuisine.

One of the defining features of Mediterranean cuisine is the prominence of olive oil. This golden elixir is not only used for cooking but also as a dressing, a dip, and a flavor enhancer. Olive oil adds a distinctive richness and depth of flavor to Mediterranean dishes, and it is a staple ingredient in the region.

Seafood, particularly fish, is another integral component of Mediterranean cuisine. With its abundant coastline, the Mediterranean region is blessed with an array of fresh fish and seafood. Grilled or baked fish, seasoned with herbs, lemon, and olive oil, is a classic Mediterranean dish that exemplifies the simplicity and elegance of the cuisine.

Herbs and spices are fundamental to Mediterranean cooking, adding layers of flavor and aroma to dishes. Commonly used herbs include basil, oregano, thyme, rosemary, and parsley, while spices like cinnamon, cumin, paprika, and saffron bring depth and complexity to the cuisine.

The Mediterranean region is also renowned for its vibrant and colorful produce. Fresh fruits and vegetables are celebrated in Mediterranean cuisine, with dishes showcasing the natural flavors and textures of ingredients such as tomatoes, eggplants, zucchini, peppers, and citrus fruits.

Furthermore, the concept of communal dining and sharing meals is deeply ingrained in Mediterranean culture. Meals are often enjoyed with family and friends, fostering a sense of togetherness and conviviality.

In conclusion, Mediterranean cuisine is a tapestry of flavors, traditions, and histories woven together by the countries surrounding the Mediterranean Sea. Its emphasis on fresh, seasonal ingredients, simple yet skillful preparation techniques, and a balanced approach to eating make it a truly remarkable culinary tradition. Whether you are indulging in a Greek moussaka, an Italian pasta dish, a Spanish paella, or a Moroccan tagine, Mediterranean cuisine offers a gastronomic journey filled with tantalizing aromas and exquisite flavors.

The Mediterranean region has a long history of trade and cultural exchange, which has greatly influenced its cuisine. The Phoenicians, Greeks, Romans, Arabs, and Ottomans, among others, have all left their mark on the culinary traditions of the Mediterranean. This rich history has resulted in a diverse range of flavors, ingredients, and cooking techniques.

In addition to olive oil, another key ingredient in Mediterranean cuisine is fresh herbs. Mediterranean countries are known for their abundant herb gardens, where herbs such as mint, thyme, oregano, and basil flourish. These herbs are used generously in various dishes, adding a fragrant and aromatic quality to the cuisine.

Cheese is also an important component of Mediterranean cuisine. Greece is famous for feta cheese, while Italy is renowned for its mozzarella and Parmesan. These cheeses are often used in salads, pasta dishes, and as toppings for pizzas, adding a creamy and savory element to the cuisine.

Bread is a staple in the Mediterranean diet, and each country has its own unique bread traditions. From the crusty baguettes of France to the pita bread of Greece and the focaccia of Italy, bread is a versatile and essential part of Mediterranean cuisine. It is often used to scoop up dips, wrap sandwiches, or accompany meals.

The concept of "mezze" is prevalent in Mediterranean cuisine. Mezze refers to a selection of small, flavorful dishes that are shared among diners. It is a social and interactive way of eating, allowing people to sample a variety of flavors and textures. Mezze can include dishes such as hummus, tabbouleh, dolmades, falafel, and tzatziki.

The Mediterranean region is also known for its sweet treats and desserts. Baklava from Greece and Turkey, gelato from Italy, and crème caramel from France are just a few examples of the delightful desserts found in the Mediterranean. These desserts often feature ingredients such as honey, nuts, citrus, and spices, creating a harmonious balance of flavors.

Mediterranean cuisine is not only delicious but also promotes a healthy and balanced lifestyle. The emphasis on fresh fruits and vegetables, whole grains, and lean proteins contributes to the nutritional value of the cuisine. The Mediterranean diet is renowned for its capacity to promote a prolonged and healthy life by decreasing the risk of chronic illnesses. Consequently, it has become increasingly popular among individuals who are looking for a nutritious eating plan.

In conclusion, Mediterranean cuisine is a mosaic of flavors, ingredients, and cultural influences. From the vibrant markets of Morocco to the coastal villages of Greece, the Mediterranean region offers a diverse and captivating culinary experience. Whether you are a fan of fresh seafood, aromatic spices, or hearty vegetables, the Mediterranean cuisine has something to satisfy every palate.

MEDITERRANEAN DIET MEAL PREP TIPS AND TRICKS

Mastering the art of meal prep is crucial to maintaining the Mediterranean lifestyle, especially for those with busy schedules. Preparing meals in advance not only saves time but also ensures you stick to your healthful eating habits. Here are some invaluable tips and tricks to help you navigate your Mediterranean diet meal prep journey.

1. **Plan before you shop**: Before heading to the grocery store, make a list that includes diverse ingredients such as whole grains, lean proteins, fruits, vegetables, and healthy fats that the Mediterranean diet encourages.

2. **Embrace batch cooking**: Preparing large portions of a recipe to last several meals or days is time-efficient and prevents resorting to unhealthy meal options due to lack of time.

3. **Invest in quality storage containers**: BPA-free containers, mason jars, and glass containers are perfect for storing prepped meals, keeping them fresh and inviting.

4. **Keep it simple**: Start with simple recipes. For instance, a salad with leafy greens, cherry tomatoes, cucumber, feta cheese, and a drizzle of olive oil is easy to prepare and packed with nutrients.

5. **Incorporate variety**: To avoid meal boredom, mix things up. Try different grains, switch up your proteins, experiment with various veggies, and explore new flavors and spices.

6. **Prep components, not just full meals**: Prepping individual components like a pot of quinoa or a tray of roasted vegetables allows you to mix and match meals throughout the week.

Remember, the goal of meal prep is to make the Mediterranean diet lifestyle manageable and enjoyable for you. With these tips and tricks at hand, you're well on your way to a healthful culinary experience.

KEY RULES FOR SHOPPING ON A MEDITERRANEAN DIET MEAL PREP

The Mediterranean diet embraces a variety of wholesome and nutritionally dense foods. To successfully adopt this lifestyle, it's essential to make informed choices while grocery shopping. Here are the main rules to guide you:

1. **Prioritize Fresh, Whole Foods**: The Mediterranean diet emphasizes fresh fruits, vegetables, whole grains, and lean proteins. Processed foods, on the other hand, should be minimized as they often contain added sugars and unhealthy fats.

2. **Choose Seasonal Produce**: Seasonal fruits and vegetables not only offer the best taste and nutritional value but also are more cost-effective and environmentally friendly.

3. **Opt for Whole Grains**: Instead of refined grains, opt for whole grains like brown rice, quinoa, and whole grain bread or pasta. They are a great source of fiber and keep you feeling full for longer.

4. **Lean Proteins are Key**: Fish, poultry, beans, and eggs are excellent sources of lean protein. Red meat should be consumed sparingly, and when you do, choose lean cuts.

5. **Don't Forget Healthy Fats**: Olive oil, avocados, nuts, seeds, and fatty fish like salmon or mackerel are rich in heart-healthy fats that are a cornerstone of the Mediterranean diet.

6. **Avoid Added Sugars**: Limit foods and beverages with high added sugars. Instead, satisfy your sweet tooth with natural sugars from fruits or a bit of honey.

7. **Spice it Up**: Herbs and spices add flavor without extra calories. They also offer various health benefits, so don't hesitate to experiment.

8. **Stay Hydrated with Water**: While the Mediterranean diet includes the occasional glass of red wine, water should be your primary beverage.

Remember, shopping with a plan and sticking to these rules will make adhering to the Mediterranean diet much more manageable and enjoyable.

CHAPTER 1
BREAKFAST
RECIPES

MUFFIN-TIN SPANAKOPITA OMELETS

- Total Cooking Time: 35 minutes
- Prep Time: 15 minutes
- Servings: 6 omelets

Ingredients:

- 2 cups fresh spinach, chopped
- 1/2 cup feta cheese, crumbled
- 1/4 cup green onions, chopped
- 1/4 cup fresh dill, chopped
- 6 large eggs
- 1/4 cup milk
- 1/4 teaspoon salt
- 1/4 teaspoon black pepper
- Cooking spray

Directions:

1. To begin, set your oven temperature to 375°F (190°C). Next, lightly coat a muffin tin with cooking spray.
2. Combine the chopped spinach, feta cheese, green onions, and fresh dill in a medium-sized bowl. Mix the ingredients together until they are well blended and evenly distributed.
3. Using a whisk, blend together the eggs, milk, salt, and black pepper in a separate bowl. Ensure that the ingredients are thoroughly combined.
4. Then, distribute the spinach mixture evenly among the muffin cups, filling them approximately halfway.
5. Gently drizzle the egg mixture over the spinach in every muffin cup, ensuring they are filled almost to the rim.
6. Gently stir the mixture in each muffin cup with a fork to ensure the ingredients are well combined.
7. Put the muffin tin into the oven that has been preheated and bake for 20-25 minutes, or until the omelets have set and developed a slight golden color on top.
8. Take out the muffin tin from the oven and allow the omelets to cool for a few minutes.
9. With the aid of a small spatula or butter knife, carefully remove the omelets from the muffin tin and delicately transfer them onto a plate for serving.
10. Serve the Muffin-Tin Spanakopita Omelets warm and enjoy!

Nutritional breakdown per serving:

Calories: 124 kcal, Protein: 10 grams, Carbohydrates: 3 grams, Fat: 8 grams, Saturated Fat: 3 grams, Cholesterol: 201 milligrams, Sodium: 328 milligrams, Fiber: 1 grams, and Sugar: 1 grams.

HOMEMADE PLAIN YOGURT

- Total Cooking Time: 8 hours (including incubation time)
- Prep Time: 5 minutes
- Servings: Varies based on the amount of milk used

Ingredients:

- 4 cups whole milk (preferably organic)
- 2 tablespoons of plain yogurt that contains live and active cultures

Directions:

1. To get started, carefully pour the entire quantity of whole milk into a large saucepan and proceed to heat it over medium-low heat. Continue heating until the milk reaches a temperature of 180°F (82°C). Remember to stir occasionally in order to avoid scorching the milk.
2. Once the milk has reached the desired temperature, gently remove the saucepan from the heat source and allow it to cool naturally until it reaches a temperature of 110°F (43°C). To expedite the cooling process, you can place the saucepan in a cold water bath.
3. To temper the yogurt starter, combine 2 tablespoons of plain yogurt with a few tablespoons of the cooled milk in a small bowl. This will facilitate a smooth blending of the yogurt starter into the milk.
4. Add the tempered yogurt mixture to the remaining cooled milk in the saucepan. Stir gently to combine.
5. Pour the milk and yogurt mixture into clean, sterilized glass jars or containers with lids.
6. Cover the jars with lids and place them in a warm spot, such as an oven with the light turned on or a countertop, to incubate. Let the yogurt culture for about 6-8 hours, or until it thickens to your desired consistency.
7. Once the yogurt has set, refrigerate it for at least 2 hours to cool and firm up before serving.
8. Serve the Homemade Plain Yogurt chilled and enjoy it as is or with your favorite toppings or mix-ins.

Nutritional breakdown per serving (1 cup)::

Calories: 149 kcal, Protein: 8 grams, Carbohydrates: 11 grams, Fat: 8 grams, Saturated Fat: 5 grams, Cholesterol: 31 milligrams, Sodium: 104 milligrams, Fiber: 0 grams, and Sugar: 12 grams.

FIG & RICOTTA TOAST

- Total Cooking Time: 10 minutes
- Prep Time: 5 minutes
- Servings: 2 toasts

Ingredients:

- 2 slices whole grain bread
- 1/2 cup ricotta cheese
- 4 fresh figs, sliced
- 1 tablespoon honey
- 1 tablespoon chopped walnuts

Directions:

1. Toast the whole grain bread slices until they turn a beautiful golden color and become delightfully crispy.
2. Evenly distribute a generous layer of ricotta cheese onto each slice of toasted bread.
3. Arrange the sliced figs on top of the ricotta, distributing them evenly.
4. Drizzle honey over the figs, ensuring they are lightly coated.
5. Sprinkle the chopped walnuts over the figs and honey, adding a delightful crunch to the toast.
6. Serve the Fig & Ricotta Toast immediately and enjoy!

Nutritional breakdown per serving (1 cup):

Calories: 245 kcal, Protein: 9 grams, Carbohydrates: 34 grams, Fat: 10 grams, Saturated Fat: 5 grams, Cholesterol: 27 milligrams, Sodium: 204 milligrams, Fiber: 4 grams, and Sugar: 17 grams.

CHERRY-WALNUT OVERNIGHT OATS

- Total Cooking Time: 8 hours (including overnight refrigeration)
- Prep Time: 5 minutes
- Servings: 2

Ingredients:

- 1 cup rolled oats
- 1 cup unsweetened almond milk
- 1/4 cup Greek yogurt
- 1 tablespoon honey (optional)
- 1/4 teaspoon vanilla extract
- 1/4 cup dried cherries
- 2 tablespoons chopped walnuts

Directions:

1. In a bowl or jar, combine the rolled oats, almond milk, Greek yogurt, honey (if desired), and vanilla extract. Carefully stir the mixture to ensure that all the ingredients are fully combined.
2. Incorporate the dried cherries and chopped walnuts into the oat mixture, ensuring they are evenly distributed by stirring once more.
3. Wrap the bowl or jar with a lid or plastic wrap to help the oats attain a tender texture and soak in the delightful flavors, then place it in the refrigerator for at least 8 hours or overnight.
4. In the morning, give the overnight oats a thorough stir. If preferred, you have the option to add a small amount of almond milk to achieve your desired consistency.
5. Divide the Cherry-Walnut Overnight Oats into two serving bowls or jars.
6. Top with additional dried cherries and chopped walnuts for garnish, if desired.
7. Serve the overnight oats chilled and enjoy!

Nutritional breakdown per serving:

Calories: 293 kcal, Protein: 9 grams, Carbohydrates: 44 grams, Fat: 10 grams, Saturated Fat: 1 grams, Cholesterol: 1 milligrams, Sodium: 83 milligrams, Fiber: 6 grams, and Sugar: 13 grams.

BAKED OMELET TOAST

- Total Cooking Time: 25 minutes
- Prep Time: 10 minutes
- Servings: 2

Ingredients:

- 4 slices whole grain bread
- 4 large eggs
- 1/4 cup milk
- Salt and pepper, to taste
- 1/4 cup diced bell peppers
- 1/4 cup diced tomatoes
- 1/4 cup diced onions
- 1/4 cup shredded cheese
- Fresh herbs, for garnish

Directions:

1. To begin the cooking process, adjust the oven temperature to 375°F (190°C).
2. To avoid any potential sticking, it is recommended to lightly coat a baking sheet with a thin layer of grease or alternatively, use parchment paper to line the sheet.
3. Position the slices of bread onto the baking sheet that has been previously prepared.
4. To create the mixture, simply combine the eggs, milk, salt, and pepper in a bowl. Whisk the ingredients together until they are fully incorporated and well blended.
5. Evenly distribute the egg mixture over the slices of bread, ensuring that it is absorbed evenly.
6. Sprinkle the diced bell peppers, tomatoes, onions, and shredded cheese over the egg-soaked bread.
7. To attain a lovely golden shade, place the warmed baking sheet in the oven and let it bake for approximately 15 to 20 minutes. It's crucial to verify that the eggs are thoroughly cooked and the cheese has melted before removing it from the oven.
8. Remove the baked omelet toast from the oven and let it cool for a few minutes.
9. Garnish with fresh herbs, if desired.
10. Slice the baked omelet toast into halves or quarters and serve warm.

Nutritional breakdown per serving:

Calories: 285 kcal, Protein: 19 grams, Carbohydrates: 25 grams, Fat: 12 grams, Saturated Fat: 4 grams, Cholesterol: 372 milligrams, Sodium: 430 milligrams, Fiber: 4 grams, and Sugar: 4 grams.

SHAKSHUKA

- Total Cooking Time: 30 minutes
- Prep Time: 10 minutes
- Servings: 4

Ingredients:

- 2 tablespoons olive oil
- 1 onion, thinly sliced
- 1 red bell pepper, thinly sliced
- 2 cloves garlic, minced
- 1 teaspoon ground cumin
- 1 teaspoon ground paprika
- 1/2 teaspoon ground cayenne pepper
- 1 can (14 ounces) crushed tomatoes
- Salt and pepper, to taste
- 4-6 large eggs
- Fresh herbs for garnish

Directions:

1. In a sizable skillet or frying pan, warm the olive oil over medium heat.
2. Cook the sliced onion and bell pepper in the pan, sautéing them until they begin to soften, typically within a span of about 5 minutes.
3. Stir in the minced garlic, ground cumin, ground paprika, and ground cayenne pepper (if using). Cook for an extra 1-2 minutes until a delightful aroma emerges.
4. To prepare the dish, carefully pour the crushed tomatoes into the pan, then season with salt and pepper according to your personal taste. To achieve a uniform blend, make sure to stir the mixture thoroughly, ensuring that all the ingredients are well incorporated.
5. Reduce the heat to low and let the tomato mixture simmer for about 10-15 minutes, allowing the flavors to meld together.
6. Create small wells in the tomato mixture and carefully crack the eggs into each well.
7. Place a lid on the pan and allow the dish to cook for approximately 5-7 minutes, or until the eggs are cooked to your preferred level of doneness. For runny yolks, cook for a shorter time, and for fully cooked yolks, cook for a longer time.
8. After taking the pan off the heat, you can add a touch of freshly chopped parsley or cilantro to give it a delightful final touch.
9. Serve the Shakshuka hot with crusty bread or pita on the side.

Nutritional breakdown per serving:

Calories: 187 kcal, Protein: 9 grams, Carbohydrates: 13 grams, Fat: 12 grams, Saturated Fat: 2 grams, Cholesterol: 186 milligrams, Sodium: 328 milligrams, Fiber: 3 grams, and Sugar: 7 grams.

CHICKPEA TOAST

- Total Cooking Time: 15 minutes
- Prep Time: 5 minutes
- Servings: 2

Ingredients:

- 1 can chickpeas, drained and rinsed
- 2 tablespoons olive oil
- 1 tablespoon lemon juice
- 1 clove garlic, minced
- 1/2 teaspoon ground cumin
- Salt and pepper, to taste
- 4 slices whole grain bread
- 1 small cucumber, thinly sliced
- Fresh herbs for garnish

Directions:

1. Combine chickpeas, olive oil, lemon juice, minced garlic, ground cumin, salt, and pepper in a food processor. Blend the ingredients until they form a smooth and creamy mixture, ensuring to scrape down the sides as needed.
2. Toast the slices of bread until golden and crispy.
3. Apply a generous layer of the chickpea mixture onto each slice of toasted bread.
4. Top the chickpea spread with thinly sliced cucumber.
5. Add a touch of fresh herbs, such as parsley or dill, to enhance the flavor.
6. Serve the Chickpea Toast as an open-faced sandwich or cut into halves or quarters.

Nutritional breakdown per serving:

Calories: 315 kcal, Protein: 12 grams, Carbohydrates: 42 grams, Fat: 12 grams, Saturated Fat: 2 grams, Cholesterol: 0 milligrams, Sodium: 420 milligrams, Fiber: 9 grams, and Sugar: 5 grams.

BREAKFAST QUINOA

- Total Cooking Time: 20 minutes
- Prep Time: 5 minutes
- Servings: 2

Ingredients:

- 1 cup quinoa
- 2 cups water
- 1 cup almond milk
- 1 tablespoon honey or maple syrup
- 1/2 teaspoon vanilla extract
- 1/2 teaspoon ground cinnamon
- 1/4 cup chopped nuts
- 1/4 cup dried fruits
- Fresh herbs for garnish

Directions:

1. Rinse the quinoa under cold water to remove any bitterness.
2. To start, place the rinsed quinoa and water in a saucepan. Apply medium heat to the mixture until it reaches the point of boiling.
3. Once the mixture has reached a boiling point, lower the heat to a low setting and tightly cover the saucepan. Allow the quinoa to simmer for approximately 15 minutes, or until it has absorbed all the water and become tender.
4. In a separate small saucepan, warm the almond milk over medium heat.
5. Blend the honey or maple syrup, vanilla extract, and ground cinnamon into the warm almond milk, stirring thoroughly.
6. After the quinoa has finished cooking, take it off the heat source and gently stir it with a fork to separate the grains.
7. Drizzle the sweetened almond milk mixture onto the cooked quinoa and thoroughly mix it to ensure everything is well incorporated.
8. Incorporate the chopped nuts and dried fruits into the mixture.
9. Divide the breakfast quinoa into serving bowls.
10. Top with fresh fruits of your choice.
11. Serve warm and enjoy!

Nutritional breakdown per serving:

Calories: 350 kcal, Protein: 10 grams, Carbohydrates: 62 grams, Fat: 8 grams, Saturated Fat: 1 grams, Cholesterol: 0 milligrams, Sodium: 20 milligrams, Fiber: 7 grams, and Sugar: 14 grams.

CHICKEN MEAL PREP

- Total Cooking Time: 40 minutes
- Prep Time: 15 minutes
- Servings: 4

Ingredients:

- 4 boneless, skinless chicken breasts
- 2 tablespoons olive oil
- 1 teaspoon dried oregano
- 1 teaspoon dried basil
- 1/2 teaspoon garlic powder
- 1/2 teaspoon onion powder
- Salt and pepper, to taste
- 4 cups mixed vegetables (such as bell peppers, zucchini, and broccoli)
- 2 cups cooked quinoa or brown rice

Directions:

1. Before commencing the preparation of your dish, it is advisable to set the oven temperature to 400°F (200°C) to ensure thorough cooking.
2. Position the chicken breasts onto a baking sheet that has been readied with parchment paper.
3. Coat the chicken breasts generously with olive oil and season them with a sprinkling of dried oregano, dried basil, garlic powder, onion powder, salt, and pepper. Massage the seasonings into the chicken to ensure an even distribution.
4. To ensure the chicken is thoroughly cooked, place the seasoned chicken in a preheated oven and bake for about 25-30 minutes, or until the internal temperature reaches 165°F (74°C).
5. As the chicken bakes, get the mixed vegetables ready by cutting them into bite-sized pieces.
6. To commence cooking, heat a tablespoon of olive oil in a generously sized skillet over medium heat.
7. Sauté the array of vegetables in the pan over medium heat for approximately 8 to 10 minutes, or until they develop a tender-crisp texture.
8. Flavor the vegetables with salt and pepper according to your preference, incorporating the desired level of seasoning.
9. Divide the cooked quinoa or brown rice into meal prep containers.
10. Cut the prepared chicken breasts into slices and place them in the containers.

11. Add the sautéed mixed vegetables to the containers.
12. Allow the chicken meal prep to cool before sealing the containers and storing them in the refrigerator.

Nutritional breakdown per serving:

Calories: 350 kcal, Protein: 35 grams, Carbohydrates: 30 grams, Fat: 10 grams, Saturated Fat: 2 grams, Cholesterol: 80 milligrams, Sodium: 150 milligrams, Fiber: 5 grams, and Sugar: 3 grams.

BAKED COD

- Total Cooking Time: 25 minutes
- Prep Time: 10 minutes
- Servings: 4

Ingredients:

- 4 cod fillets (about 6 ounces each)
- 2 tablespoons olive oil
- 2 cloves garlic, minced
- 1 teaspoon dried oregano
- 1/2 teaspoon dried thyme
- 1/2 teaspoon paprika
- Salt and pepper, to taste
- Lemon wedges, for serving
- Fresh parsley, chopped (for garnish)

Directions:

1. Before beginning the preparation of your dish, it is advisable to set the oven temperature to 400°F (200°C) to ensure thorough cooking.
2. Position the cod fillets on a baking sheet that has been prepared with a layer of parchment paper.
3. In a small bowl, combine the olive oil, minced garlic, dried oregano, dried thyme, paprika, salt, and pepper. Stir well to make a marinade.
4. Brush the marinade over the cod fillets, coating them evenly on both sides.
5. Cook the cod in the preheated oven for approximately 15 minutes, or until the fish becomes opaque and easily flakes apart when prodded with a fork.
6. Let the baked cod rest for a few minutes after removing it from the oven.
7. Present the cod with lemon wedges on the side, allowing the option to squeeze the lemon over the fish.
8. Garnish with freshly chopped parsley.
9. Savor the Baked Cod as the main course, pairing it with your preferred sides, like roasted vegetables or a salad.

Nutritional breakdown per serving:

Calories: 180 kcal, Protein: 28 grams, Carbohydrates: 1 grams, Fat: 7 grams, Saturated Fat: 1 grams, Cholesterol: 70 milligrams, Sodium: 200 milligrams, Fiber: 0 grams, and Sugar: 0 grams.

GREEK YOGURT PARFAIT

- Total Cooking Time: 5 minutes
- Prep Time: 5 minutes
- Servings: 1

Ingredients:

- 1 cup Greek yogurt
- 1/2 cup mixed berries
- 2 tablespoons honey or maple syrup
- 2 tablespoons granola
- 1 tablespoon chopped nuts
- Fresh mint leaves, for garnish (optional)

Directions:

1. In a serving glass or bowl, layer half of the Greek yogurt.
2. Add half of the mixed berries on top of the yogurt.
3. Pour a tablespoon of honey or maple syrup onto the berries.
4. Sprinkle 1 tablespoon of granola and 1/2 tablespoon of chopped nuts over the berries.
5. Repeat the layers with the remaining Greek yogurt, mixed berries, honey or maple syrup, granola, and chopped nuts.
6. Garnish with fresh mint leaves, if desired.
7. Serve the Greek Yogurt Parfait immediately or refrigerate for later consumption.

Nutritional breakdown per serving:

Calories: 250 kcal, Protein: 15 grams, Carbohydrates: 35 grams, Fat: 6 grams, Saturated Fat: 1 grams, Cholesterol: 10 milligrams, Sodium: 60 milligrams, Fiber: 4 grams, and Sugar: 26 grams.

VEGETABLE FRITTATA

- Total Cooking Time: 30 minutes
- Prep Time: 15 minutes
- Servings: 4

Ingredients:

- 6 large eggs
- 1/4 cup milk
- 1 tablespoon olive oil
- 1 small onion, diced
- 1 bell pepper, diced
- 1 zucchini, diced
- 1 cup cherry tomatoes, halved
- 1/2 cup crumbled feta cheese
- 2 tablespoons chopped fresh herbs
- Salt and pepper, to taste

Directions:

1. Before you begin using the oven, make sure to set it to a temperature of 375°F (190°C).
2. In a bowl for mixing, combine the eggs and milk by whisking them together. Keep the mixture aside for later use.
3. To begin, warm up the olive oil in a skillet that is safe to use in the oven. Use medium heat for this step.
4. Add the diced onion, bell pepper, and zucchini to the skillet. Sauté for about 5 minutes, or until the vegetables are tender.
5. Incorporate the cherry tomatoes into the skillet and continue cooking for an additional 2 minutes.
6. To elevate the flavor of the vegetables, add salt and pepper to your preferred level of seasoning.
7. Pour the egg mixture over the sautéed vegetables in the skillet.
8. Distribute the crumbled feta cheese evenly across the surface.
9. Cook the frittata over medium heat for 3-4 minutes, or until the edges begin to firm up.
10. Move the skillet to the preheated oven and let it bake for about 15 to 18 minutes, or until the frittata is cooked through in the center and has a light golden color on the surface.

11. After removing the frittata from the oven, it is recommended to let it cool for a brief period before serving.
12. Sprinkle the chopped fresh herbs over the frittata.
13. Cut the frittata into wedges and enjoy it while it's warm.

Nutritional breakdown per serving:

Calories: 180 kcal, Protein: 12 grams, Carbohydrates: 9 grams, Fat: 11 grams, Saturated Fat: 4 grams, Cholesterol: 280 milligrams, Sodium: 320 milligrams, Fiber: 2 grams, and Sugar: 5 grams.

GREEK SPINACH AND FETA MUFFINS

- Total Cooking Time: 30 minutes
- Prep Time: 15 minutes
- Servings: 4

Ingredients:

- 1 tablespoon olive oil
- 1 small onion, finely chopped
- 2 cups fresh spinach, chopped
- 1/2 cup crumbled feta cheese
- 1/4 cup chopped fresh herbs
- 4 large eggs
- 1/4 cup milk
- Salt and pepper, to taste

Directions:

1. Commence by warming your oven to 375°F (190°C). Afterward, you can choose to either grease a muffin tin or utilize muffin liners.
2. To start, warm the olive oil in a skillet over medium heat. Afterward, incorporate the diced onion into the skillet and continue cooking until it reaches a translucent state, usually requiring approximately 3 to 4 minutes.
3. Next, introduce the chopped spinach to the skillet and cook until it wilts, which should take approximately 2 to 3 minutes. Subsequently, remove the skillet from the heat source and allow the spinach to cool slightly.
4. In a bowl used for mixing, combine the eggs and milk using a whisk. It is crucial to add salt and pepper to the mixture to elevate the taste.
5. Add the cooked spinach, crumbled feta cheese, and chopped fresh herbs to the egg mixture. Stir well to combine.
6. Distribute the mixture evenly into the prepared muffin tin, making sure that each cup is filled to about three-fourths of its capacity.
7. To start, place the muffin tin into the oven that has been preheated and bake for approximately 15 to 18 minutes. Keep an eye on them and remove them from the oven when they are firm and have a light golden color on top.
8. Let the muffins cool in the tin for a brief period once they have been taken out of the oven.
9. Gently take out the muffins from the tin and serve them while they are still warm.

Nutritional breakdown per serving:

Calories: 150 kcal, Protein: 10 grams, Carbohydrates: 5 grams, Fat: 10 grams, Saturated Fat: 4 grams, Cholesterol: 190 milligrams, Sodium: 280 milligrams, Fiber: 1 grams, and Sugar: 2 grams.

AVOCADO TOAST

- Total Cooking Time: 10 minutes
- Prep Time: 5 minutes
- Servings: 2

Ingredients:

- 2 slices whole grain bread
- 1 ripe avocado
- 1 small tomato, sliced
- 1/4 cup crumbled feta cheese
- Fresh basil leaves, for garnish
- Salt and pepper, to taste
- Lemon juice (optional)

Directions:

1. Toast the slices of whole grain bread to your desired level of crispness.
2. As the bread is being toasted, take the avocado and slice it in half. Be cautious as you remove the pit from the avocado. After successfully removing the pit, utilize a spoon to scoop out the creamy avocado flesh and transfer it into a small bowl.
3. Gently mash the avocado with a fork until it reaches the desired consistency. If you like, you can season it with salt and pepper to suit your taste. To enhance the taste, you may want to try incorporating a fresh lemon juice squeeze for an added burst of flavor.
4. After toasting the bread, ensure to spread the mashed avocado evenly on each slice.
5. Top the avocado with sliced tomatoes and crumbled feta cheese.
6. Garnish with fresh basil leaves.
7. Serve the Mediterranean Avocado Toast immediately.

Nutritional breakdown per serving:

Calories: 220 kcal, Protein: 8 grams, Carbohydrates: 24 grams, Fat: 12 grams, Saturated Fat: 3 grams, Cholesterol: 10 milligrams, Sodium: 320 milligrams, Fiber: 7 grams, and Sugar: 3 grams.

GREEK YOGURT PANCAKES

- Total Cooking Time: 20 minutes
- Prep Time: 10 minutes
- Servings: 2-3

Ingredients:

- 1 cup all-purpose flour
- 1 tablespoon sugar
- 1 teaspoon baking powder
- 1/2 teaspoon baking soda
- 1/4 teaspoon salt
- 1 cup Greek yogurt
- 1/4 cup milk
- 1 large egg
- 1 tablespoon melted butter
- 1 teaspoon vanilla extract
- Fresh berries, for serving
- Honey or maple syrup, for serving

Directions:

1. In a mixing bowl, combine the flour, sugar, baking powder, baking soda, and salt. Utilize a whisk to meticulously combine the ingredients until they are completely integrated.
2. In a separate bowl, combine the Greek yogurt, milk, egg, melted butter, and vanilla extract. Whisk until well combined.
3. Delicately pour the liquid ingredients into the dry components and softly combine them until they are thoroughly mixed. Remember to avoid overmixing the batter; a few lumps are acceptable and won't affect the final result.
4. Warm up a non-stick skillet or griddle over medium heat before use. To ensure a light greasing, you can either apply a thin coating of cooking spray or a small amount of butter to the surface.
5. When making each pancake, pour 1/4 cup of batter onto the skillet. Once bubbles begin to form on the surface of the pancake, it is time to delicately flip it over. Cook for another 1-2 minutes, or until the pancake develops a pleasing golden brown hue.
6. Proceed with the remaining batter by repeating the same steps, ensuring to apply more cooking spray or butter if required.

7. Enjoy the Greek Yogurt Pancakes while they are warm, and enhance their flavor by garnishing them with a generous serving of fresh berries and a delightful drizzle of honey or maple syrup.

Nutritional breakdown per serving:

Calories (2 pancakes): 280 kcal, Protein: 12 grams, Carbohydrates: 43 grams, Fat: 7 grams, Saturated Fat: 4 grams, Cholesterol: 65 milligrams, Sodium: 520 milligrams, Fiber: 1 grams, and Sugar: 9 grams.

MEDITERRANEAN EGG WRAPS

- Total Cooking Time: 15 minutes
- Prep Time: 10 minutes
- Servings: 2

Ingredients:

- 4 large eggs
- 1/4 cup diced tomatoes
- 1/4 cup diced cucumbers
- 1/4 cup chopped Kalamata olives
- 1/4 cup crumbled feta cheese
- 2 tablespoons chopped fresh herbs
- Salt and pepper, to taste
- 2 large whole wheat tortillas

Directions:

1. Using a bowl, vigorously whisk the eggs until they are fully beaten. To enhance the flavor, sprinkle a small amount of salt and pepper.
2. Place a non-stick skillet on the stove and heat it over a medium flame. Gently transfer the beaten eggs into the skillet and cook them, stirring occasionally, until they transform into fluffy scrambled eggs and are cooked thoroughly. Take the skillet off the heat.
3. Lay out the whole wheat tortillas on a clean surface.
4. Evenly distribute the scrambled eggs among the tortillas, spreading them in a line down the center.
5. Garnish the eggs with chopped tomatoes, cucumbers, Kalamata olives, crumbled feta cheese, and freshly chopped herbs.
6. First, fold the sides of the tortillas over the filling, then tightly roll them up to create wraps.
7. Cut the wraps in half diagonally and serve.

Nutritional breakdown per serving:

Calories:320 kcal, Protein: 20 grams, Carbohydrates: 22 grams, Fat: 18 grams, Saturated Fat: 6 grams, Cholesterol: 380 milligrams, Sodium: 660 milligrams, Fiber: 4 grams, and Sugar: 3 grams.

TOFU SCRAMBLE WITH SPINACH AND MUSHROOMS

- Total Cooking Time: 15 minutes
- Prep Time: 10 minutes
- Servings: 2

Ingredients:

- 1 tablespoon olive oil
- 1/2 onion, diced
- 2 cloves garlic, minced
- 8 ounces firm tofu, drained and crumbled
- 1 cup sliced mushrooms
- 2 cups fresh spinach
- 1 teaspoon turmeric
- 1/2 teaspoon cumin
- 1/2 teaspoon paprika
- Salt and pepper, to taste
- Fresh parsley, for garnish (optional)

Directions:

1. Begin by placing the skillet over medium heat and warming the olive oil until it reaches a warm temperature.
2. Place the diced onion and minced garlic into the skillet. Sauté them until the onion turns translucent.
3. Place the crumbled tofu in the skillet and cook for 2-3 minutes, stirring occasionally.
4. Transfer the sliced mushrooms into the skillet and proceed to cook them for an extra 3-4 minutes, or until they reach a state of softness and tenderness.
5. Incorporate the fresh spinach into the mixture and continue cooking until it wilts.
6. Sprinkle turmeric, cumin, paprika, salt, and pepper over the tofu mixture. Thoroughly mix the ingredients together and continue to cook for a duration of 1-2 minutes.
7. Remove the skillet from heat.
8. Serve the tofu scramble hot, garnished with fresh parsley if desired.

Nutritional breakdown per serving:

Calories: 180 kcal, Protein: 14 grams, Carbohydrates: 9 grams, Fat: 10 grams, Saturated Fat: 1.5 grams, Cholesterol: 0 milligrams, Sodium: 190 milligrams, Fiber: 3 grams, and Sugar: 2 grams.

BREAKFAST BURRITOGREEK OMELETTE

- Total Cooking Time: 10 minutes
- Prep Time: 5 minutes
- Servings: 1

Ingredients:

- 2 large eggs
- 1/4 cup diced tomatoes
- 1/4 cup diced cucumbers
- 2 tablespoons chopped Kalamata olives
- 2 tablespoons crumbled feta cheese
- 1 tablespoon chopped fresh herbs
- Salt and pepper, to taste
- 1 large whole wheat tortilla

Directions:

1. In a bowl, vigorously whisk the eggs until they are thoroughly beaten. Gently sprinkle a small amount of salt and pepper to add flavor to the dish.
2. To bring the non-stick skillet to a warm temperature, apply medium heat and allow it to heat up. After pouring the beaten eggs into the skillet, cook them while stirring occasionally until they are fully scrambled and reach your desired consistency. Next, remove the skillet from the heat source.
3. Lay out the whole wheat tortilla on a clean surface.
4. Spread the scrambled eggs evenly on the tortilla, leaving a border around the edges.
5. Garnish the eggs with chopped tomatoes, cucumbers, Kalamata olives, crumbled feta cheese, and freshly chopped herbs.
6. First, fold the edges of the tortilla over the filling, then tightly roll it to create a wrap.
7. Take it out of the oven and allow it to cool for a few minutes before cutting and serving.

Nutritional breakdown per serving:

Calories: 320 kcal, Protein: 20 grams, Carbohydrates: 22 grams, Fat: 18 grams, Saturated Fat: 6 grams, Cholesterol: 380 milligrams, Sodium: 660 milligrams, Fiber: 4 grams, and Sugar: 3 grams.

BREAKFAST QUICHE

- Total Cooking Time: 45 minutes
- Prep Time: 15 minutes
- Servings: 4

Ingredients:

- 1 pre-made whole wheat pie crust
- 4 large eggs
- 1/2 cup Greek yogurt
- 1/4 cup milk
- 1/2 cup diced tomatoes
- 1/2 cup chopped spinach
- 1/4 cup sliced Kalamata olives
- 1/4 cup crumbled feta cheese
- 2 tablespoons chopped fresh herbs
- Salt and pepper, to taste

Directions:

1. To begin, make sure to set the oven temperature to 375°F (190°C) before you begin utilizing it.
2. Place the pre-made whole wheat pie crust in a pie dish and set aside.
3. To start, combine the eggs, Greek yogurt, and milk in a bowl and whisk them together until they are thoroughly mixed. Ensure to add salt and pepper according to your taste preference.
4. Include the diced tomatoes, chopped spinach, sliced Kalamata olives, crumbled feta cheese, and freshly chopped herbs into the egg mixture. Continuously mix the ingredients until they are thoroughly combined.
5. Carefully transfer the egg mixture into the pie crust that has been prepared.
6. Put the quiche into the oven that has been preheated and bake it for approximately 30-35 minutes, or until the center is firm and the top has a beautiful golden brown color.
7. Take out the quiche from the oven and allow it to cool for a brief period before cutting and serving.

Nutritional breakdown per serving:

Calories: 280 kcal, Protein: 14 grams, Carbohydrates: 20 grams, Fat: 16 grams, Saturated Fat: 6 grams, Cholesterol: 190 milligrams, Sodium: 480 milligrams, Fiber: 3 grams, and Sugar: 3 grams.

CHAPTER 2
LUNCH RECIPES

GREEK SALAD WITH GRILLED CHICKEN

- Total Cooking Time: 25 minutes
- Prep Time: 15 minutes
- Servings: 4

Ingredients:

- 2 boneless, skinless chicken breasts
- 2 tablespoons extra virgin olive oil
- 1 teaspoon dried oregano
- Salt and pepper, to taste
- 4 cups mixed salad greens
- 1 cup cherry tomatoes, halved
- 1 cucumber, sliced
- 1/2 red onion, thinly sliced
- 1/2 cup of pitted and halved Kalamata olives
- 1/2 cup crumbled feta cheese
- Juice of 1 lemon
- 2 tablespoons red wine vinegar
- 1 tablespoon fresh dill, chopped

Directions:

1. Before starting, heat up a grill or grill pan on medium-high heat.
2. To prepare, bring water or vegetable broth to a boil in a medium saucepan. Add the quinoa, then lower the heat, cover, and let it simmer for approximately 15 minutes until the liquid is absorbed and the quinoa becomes tender.
3. Cook the chicken breasts on the grill for approximately 6-8 minutes on each side, or until they are fully cooked and the juices run clear. Once done, take them off the heat and allow them to rest for a few minutes before slicing.
4. Combine the cooked quinoa, cherry tomatoes, cucumber, red bell pepper, red onion, Kalamata olives, parsley, and mint in a spacious salad bowl to prepare the salad.
5. To create the dressing, blend together the lemon juice, extra virgin olive oil, salt, and pepper in a small bowl until thoroughly combined. Drizzle the dressing evenly over the quinoa mixture and delicately toss to thoroughly mix all the ingredients together.
6. Divide the salad among serving plates. Top each plate with sliced grilled chicken.
7. Serve the Greek salad with grilled chicken immediately.

Nutritional breakdown per serving:

Calories: 290 kcal, Protein: 27 grams, Carbohydrates: 12 grams, Fat: 15 grams, Saturated Fat: 7 grams, Cholesterol: 75 milligrams, Sodium: 480 milligrams, Fiber: 3 grams, and Sugar: 5 grams.

QUINOA SALAD

- Total Cooking Time: 25 minutes
- Prep Time: 15 minutes
- Servings: 4

Ingredients:

- 1 cup quinoa
- 2 cups water or vegetable broth
- 1 cup cherry tomatoes, halved
- 1 cucumber, diced
- 1 red bell pepper, diced
- 1/4 red onion, finely chopped
- 1/2 cup of Kalamata olives, with the pits removed and cut into halves
- 1/4 cup fresh parsley, chopped
- 1/4 cup fresh mint, chopped
- Juice of 1 lemon
- 2 tablespoons extra virgin olive oil
- Salt and pepper, to taste
- Optional: crumbled feta cheese for garnish (not included in nutritional value)

Directions:

1. Rinse the quinoa under cold water to remove any bitterness.
2. To prepare, bring water or vegetable broth to a boil in a medium saucepan. Add the quinoa, then lower the heat, cover, and let it simmer for approximately 15 minutes until the liquid is absorbed and the quinoa becomes tender.
3. Take the quinoa off the heat and allow it to cool for a few minutes.
4. Combine the cooked quinoa, cherry tomatoes, cucumber, red bell pepper, red onion, Kalamata olives, parsley, and mint in a large salad bowl to make the salad.
5. In a small bowl, mix the lemon juice, extra virgin olive oil, salt, and pepper thoroughly to create the dressing. Then, drizzle the dressing evenly over the quinoa mixture and gently toss to ensure all the ingredients are thoroughly mixed together.
6. If you like, you can sprinkle crumbled feta cheese over the dish just before serving.
7. To elevate the taste, it is advised to cover the salad and refrigerate it for at least 1 hour. Allowing the ingredients to meld together will create a cohesive and well-balanced blend of flavors.
8. Prior to presentation, add crumbled feta cheese as a garnish, if preferred.

Nutritional breakdown per serving:

Calories: 220 kcal, Protein: 6 grams, Carbohydrates: 31 grams, Fat: 9 grams, Saturated Fat: 1 grams, Cholesterol: 0 milligrams, Sodium: 240 milligrams, Fiber: 5 grams, and Sugar: 3 grams.

LEMON HERB SALMON WITH ROASTED VEGETABLES

- Total Cooking Time: 30 minutes
- Prep Time: 15 minutes
- Servings: 4

Ingredients:

- 4 salmon fillets (about 6 ounces each)
- 2 tablespoons extra virgin olive oil
- Zest of 1 lemon
- 2 tablespoons fresh lemon juice
- 2 cloves garlic, minced
- 1 tablespoon fresh dill, chopped
- 1 tablespoon fresh parsley, chopped
- Salt and pepper, to taste
- 4 cups mixed vegetables (such as bell peppers, zucchini, and cherry tomatoes), chopped
- 1 tablespoon balsamic vinegar

Directions:

1. Prior to commencing the baking process, it is advisable to preheat the oven to 425°F (220°C) to ensure optimal baking results.
2. Take a small bowl and mix together the olive oil, lemon zest, lemon juice, minced garlic, dill, parsley, salt, and pepper. Stir the ingredients thoroughly until they are completely combined.
3. Place the salmon fillets in a shallow container, pour the marinade over them, and allow the fillets to marinate for approximately 10 minutes.
4. In a separate bowl, carefully toss the mixed vegetables with olive oil, balsamic vinegar, salt, and pepper to ensure that all the flavors are fully blended.
5. Transfer the marinated salmon fillets to a baking sheet lined with parchment paper. Arrange the seasoned vegetables around the salmon.
6. Bake in the oven that has been preheated for about 15 minutes, or until the salmon is thoroughly cooked and the vegetables reach the desired tenderness.
7. After taking it out of the oven, allow it to rest for a few minutes before serving.
8. Serve the lemon herb salmon with roasted vegetables hot.

Nutritional breakdown per serving:

Calories: 350 kcal, Protein: 35 grams, Carbohydrates: 10 grams, Fat: 20 grams, Saturated Fat: 3.5 grams, Cholesterol: 80 milligrams, Sodium: 150 milligrams, Fiber: 3 grams, and Sugar: 4 grams.

CHICKPEA AND VEGETABLE STEW

- Total Cooking Time: 40 minutes
- Prep Time: 15 minutes
- Servings: 4

Ingredients:

- 2 tablespoons olive oil
- 1 onion, chopped
- 2 cloves garlic, minced
- 1 red bell pepper, chopped
- 1 zucchini, chopped
- 1 carrot, chopped
- 1 can (14 ounces) diced tomatoes
- 2 cups vegetable broth
- 1 teaspoon dried oregano
- 1 teaspoon dried basil
- 1/2 teaspoon paprika
- 1/4 teaspoon cayenne pepper (optional)
- 2 cans chickpeas, drained and rinsed
- Salt and pepper, to taste
- Fresh parsley, for garnish (optional)

Directions:

1. Start by placing the large pot over medium heat and heating the olive oil until it reaches a warm temperature.
2. Combine the chopped onion and minced garlic in the pot. Sauté the mixture until the onion turns translucent.
3. Add the chopped red bell pepper, zucchini, and carrot to the pot. Cook for about 5 minutes, or until the vegetables start to soften.
4. Stir in the diced tomatoes, vegetable broth, dried oregano, dried basil, paprika, and cayenne pepper (if using). Bring the mixture to a boil.
5. Lower the heat to a low setting and include the drained and rinsed chickpeas in the pot. Allow the mixture to simmer for approximately 15-20 minutes, or until both the vegetables are tender and the flavors have blended harmoniously.
6. Customize the flavor by adding salt and pepper to your preferred taste.
7. Serve the chickpea and vegetable stew hot, garnished with fresh parsley if desired.

Nutritional breakdown per serving:

Calories: 280 kcal, Protein: 12 grams, Carbohydrates: 43 grams, Fat: 8 grams, Saturated Fat: 1 grams, Cholesterol: 0 milligrams, Sodium: 700 milligrams, Fiber: 12 grams, and Sugar: 9 grams.

GRILLED VEGETABLE WRAPS WITH HUMMUS

- Total Cooking Time: 25 minutes
- Prep Time: 15 minutes
- Servings: 4

Ingredients:

- 2 zucchinis, sliced lengthwise
- 1 red bell pepper, sliced
- 1 yellow bell pepper, sliced
- 1 eggplant, sliced
- 2 tablespoons olive oil
- Salt and pepper, to taste
- 4 whole wheat tortillas
- 1 cup hummus
- Fresh basil leaves, for garnish (optional)

Directions:

1. Get your grill or grill pan ready by preheating it over medium-high heat.
2. In a bowl, toss the zucchini, red bell pepper, yellow bell pepper, and eggplant slices with olive oil, salt, and pepper.
3. Grill the vegetables for about 3-4 minutes per side, or until they are tender and have grill marks.
4. Take the vegetables off the grill and allow them to cool down a bit.
5. Generously apply hummus onto every whole wheat tortilla.
6. Place a few slices of grilled vegetables onto each tortilla.
7. Roll up the tortillas tightly, tucking in the sides as you go.
8. Slice the wraps in half and secure with toothpicks if desired.
9. Serve the grilled vegetable wraps with hummus immediately, garnished with fresh basil leaves if desired.

Nutritional breakdown per serving:

Calories: 280 kcal, Protein: 9 grams, Carbohydrates: 36 grams, Fat: 12 grams, Saturated Fat: 2 grams, Cholesterol: 0 milligrams, Sodium: 480 milligrams, Fiber: 8 grams, and Sugar: 6 grams.

GREEK LEMON CHICKEN SKEWERS WITH TZATZIKI SAUCE

- Total Cooking Time: 25 minutes
- Prep Time: 15 minutes
- Servings: 4

Ingredients: For the Chicken Skewers:

- 1.5 pounds of boneless, skinless chicken breasts, cubed
- 2 tablespoons olive oil
- Zest and juice of 1 lemon
- 2 cloves garlic, minced
- 1 teaspoon dried oregano
- Salt and pepper, to taste
- Let the wooden skewers soak in water for 30 minutes

For the Tzatziki Sauce:

- 1 cup Greek yogurt
- Grate and squeeze half a cucumber to remove excess moisture
- 1 clove garlic, minced
- 1 tablespoon fresh lemon juice
- 1 tablespoon fresh dill, chopped
- Salt and pepper, to taste

For Serving:

- Whole wheat pita bread
- Sliced tomatoes
- Sliced red onions
- Fresh parsley, for garnish (optional)

Directions:

1. Mix together olive oil, lemon zest, lemon juice, minced garlic, dried oregano, salt, and pepper in a bowl. Place the chicken cubes into the mixture and gently toss until they are evenly coated. Let the chicken marinate for at least 10 minutes.
2. Before cooking, preheat the grill or grill pan over medium-high heat.
3. String the marinated chicken cubes onto the soaked wooden skewers.

4. Grill the chicken skewers for about 4-5 minutes per side, or until cooked through and slightly charred.
5. As the chicken grills, begin preparing the tzatziki sauce. In a bowl, combine the Greek yogurt, grated cucumber, minced garlic, lemon juice, chopped dill, salt, and pepper. Stir well to combine.
6. Warm the whole wheat pita bread on the grill for a few seconds on each side.
7. Serve the grilled chicken skewers with whole wheat pita bread, sliced tomatoes, sliced red onions, and a dollop of tzatziki sauce. Garnish with fresh parsley if desired.

Nutritional breakdown per serving:

Calories: 320 kcal, Protein: 37 grams, Carbohydrates: 15 grams, Fat: 12 grams, Saturated Fat: 2 grams, Cholesterol: 90 milligrams, Sodium: 220 milligrams, Fiber: 2 grams, and Sugar: 5 grams.

MEDITERRANEAN COUSCOUS SALAD

- Total Cooking Time: 20 minutes
- Prep Time: 15 minutes
- Servings: 4

Ingredients:

- 1 cup couscous
- 1 cup boiling water
- 1 tablespoon olive oil
- 1 cucumber, diced
- 1 red bell pepper, diced
- 1/4 red onion, finely chopped
- 1/2 cup cherry tomatoes, halved
- 1/4 cup pitted Kalamata olives, halved
- 1/4 cup fresh parsley, chopped
- 1/4 cup fresh mint, chopped
- Juice of 1 lemon
- 2 tablespoons extra virgin olive oil
- Salt and pepper, to taste
- Optional: crumbled feta cheese for garnish (not included in nutritional value)

Directions:

1. Place the couscous in a large bowl. To prepare the couscous, pour boiling water over it, cover it, and let it sit for around 5 minutes or until all the water is absorbed.
2. Separate the grains of the couscous by fluffing it with a fork.
3. Combine the diced cucumber, red bell pepper, red onion, cherry tomatoes, Kalamata olives, parsley, and mint in a separate bowl, stirring them together.
4. Combine the lemon juice, extra virgin olive oil, salt, and pepper in a small bowl, then use a whisk to mix them together. Afterward, pour the dressing evenly over the vegetable mixture and gently toss to coat the vegetables, ensuring they are well-incorporated.
5. Add the vegetable mixture to the fluffed couscous and toss gently to combine.
6. Taste and adjust the seasonings as desired.
7. Chill the covered salad in a container for a minimum of 1 hour to enable the flavors to meld together.
8. Prior to serving, you can add crumbled feta cheese as a garnish, if preferred.

Nutritional breakdown per serving:

Calories: 220 kcal, Protein: 5 grams, Carbohydrates: .32 grams, Fat: 8 grams, Saturated Fat: 1 grams, Cholesterol: 0 milligrams, Sodium: 240 milligrams, Fiber: 4 grams, and Sugar: 3 grams.

FALAFEL WITH TAHINI SAUCE

- Total Cooking Time: 40 minutes
- Prep Time: 25 minutes
- Servings: 4

Ingredients: For the Falafel:

- 1 cup dried chickpeas
- 1/2 cup fresh parsley, chopped
- 1/2 cup fresh cilantro, chopped
- 1 small onion, chopped
- 3 cloves garlic, minced
- 1 teaspoon ground cumin
- 1 teaspoon ground coriander
- 1/2 teaspoon baking soda
- Salt and pepper, to taste
- Vegetable oil, for frying

For the Tahini Sauce:

- 1/2 cup tahini
- 2 tablespoons fresh lemon juice
- 2 tablespoons water
- 1 clove garlic, minced
- Salt, to taste

For Serving:

- Pita bread
- Sliced tomatoes
- Sliced cucumbers
- Sliced red onions
- Fresh parsley, for garnish (optional)

Directions:

1. Take a bowl and place the dried chickpeas in it, covering them with water. Allow the chickpeas to soak overnight. Prior to using, make sure to drain and rinse the chickpeas thoroughly.
2. In a food processor, combine the soaked chickpeas, chopped parsley, chopped cilantro, chopped onion, minced garlic, ground cumin, ground coriander, baking soda, salt, and pepper. Pulse until the mixture is well combined and forms a coarse paste.
3. Move the falafel mixture into a bowl and place it in the refrigerator for 15 minutes to allow it to solidify.
4. As the falafel mixture chills, get ready to prepare the tahini sauce. In a small bowl, whisk together the tahini, fresh lemon juice, water, minced garlic, and salt until smooth. Set aside.
5. Start the cooking process by warming the vegetable oil in a deep pan or skillet over medium heat.
6. Shape the falafel mixture into small patties or balls, about 1-2 inches in diameter.
7. Cook the falafel in batches until they achieve a golden brown and crispy texture, typically taking around 3-4 minutes on each side. To remove any excess oil, transfer the cooked food onto a plate that has been lined with paper towels.
8. Warm the pita bread in a toaster or on a grill.
9. To serve, spread some tahini sauce on the pita bread. Add falafel, sliced tomatoes, sliced cucumbers, and sliced red onions. Garnish with fresh parsley if desired.
10. Enjoy the falafel with tahini sauce immediately.

Nutritional breakdown per serving:

Calories: 380 kcal, Protein: 14 grams, Carbohydrates: 40 grams, Fat: 20 grams, Saturated Fat: 2 grams, Cholesterol: 0 milligrams, Sodium: 350 milligrams, Fiber: 10 grams, and Sugar: 4 grams.

CAPRESE SALAD WITH BALSAMIC GLAZE

- Total Cooking Time: 10 minutes
- Prep Time: 10 minutes
- Servings: 4

Ingredients:

- 4 large ripe tomatoes, sliced
- 8 ounces fresh mozzarella cheese, sliced
- Fresh basil leaves
- 2 tablespoons balsamic glaze
- 2 tablespoons extra virgin olive oil
- Salt and pepper, to taste

Directions:

1. Place the tomato slices and mozzarella slices on a serving platter, alternating them.
2. Insert fresh basil leaves between the tomato and mozzarella slices.
3. Pour the balsamic glaze and extra virgin olive oil onto the salad.
4. Adjust the seasoning of the dish with salt and pepper to suit your own flavor preferences.
5. Serve the Caprese salad immediately as a refreshing appetizer or side dish.

Nutritional breakdown per serving:

Calories: 220 kcal, Protein: 12 grams, Carbohydrates: 40 grams, Fat: 16 grams, Saturated Fat: 7 grams, Cholesterol: 40 milligrams, Sodium: 300 milligrams, Fiber: 1 grams, and Sugar: 4 grams.

GREEK LENTIL SOUP

- Total Cooking Time: 45 minutes
- Prep Time: 15 minutes
- Servings: 4

Ingredients:

- 1 cup dried lentils
- 1 onion, chopped
- 2 carrots, diced
- 2 celery stalks, diced
- 3 cloves garlic, minced
- 1 can (14 ounces) diced tomatoes
- 4 cups vegetable broth
- 1 teaspoon dried oregano
- 1 teaspoon dried thyme
- 1 bay leaf
- Salt and pepper, to taste
- Fresh lemon juice, for serving
- Fresh parsley, for garnish (optional)

Directions:

1. Rinse the lentils under cold water and remove any debris or stones.
2. Using a large pot, warm up olive oil over medium heat. Add the chopped onion, diced carrots, and diced celery. Sauté until the vegetables are softened, about 5 minutes.
3. Include the minced garlic and continue cooking for one more minute.
4. Stir in the diced tomatoes, dried oregano, dried thyme, bay leaf, salt, and pepper.
5. Add the rinsed lentils and vegetable broth to the pot. Bring the mixture to a boil.
6. To reduce the temperature to a low simmer, place a lid on the pot, and allow it to cook for around 30 minutes, or until the lentils have reached the desired softness.
7. Remove the bay leaf from the soup.
8. Taste and adjust the seasonings as desired.
9. Serve the Greek lentil soup hot, squeezing fresh lemon juice over each serving. Garnish with fresh parsley if desired.

Nutritional breakdown per serving:

Calories: 220 kcal, Protein: 14 grams, Carbohydrates: 42 grams, Fat: 1 grams, Saturated Fat: 0 grams, Cholesterol: 0 milligrams, Sodium: 800 milligrams, Fiber: 16 grams, and Sugar: 7 grams.

PASTA SALAD WITH SUN-DRIED TOMATOES AND OLIVES

- Total Cooking Time: 20 minutes
- Prep Time: 10 minutes
- Servings: 4

Ingredients:

- 8 ounces pasta (such as fusilli or penne)
- 1/2 cup sun-dried tomatoes, drained and chopped
- 1/2 cup pitted Kalamata olives, halved
- 1/4 cup red onion, thinly sliced
- 1/4 cup fresh basil leaves, chopped
- 2 tablespoons extra virgin olive oil
- 2 tablespoons balsamic vinegar
- Salt and pepper, to taste
- Optional: crumbled feta cheese for garnish (not included in nutritional value)

Directions:

1. To achieve the perfect al dente texture, adhere to the directions on the packaging for cooking the pasta. Then, proceed to drain and rinse it with cold water to cool.
2. Combine the cooked pasta with sun-dried tomatoes, Kalamata olives, red onion, and fresh basil leaves in a spacious mixing bowl.
3. Combine the extra virgin olive oil, balsamic vinegar, salt, and pepper in a small bowl, using a whisk to blend them together.
4. Delicately pour the dressing over the pasta salad and gently mix until all the ingredients are uniformly coated.
5. Taste and adjust the seasonings as desired.
6. You can serve the pasta salad either chilled or at room temperature.
7. If desired, garnish with crumbled feta cheese before serving.

Nutritional breakdown per serving:

Calories: 320 kcal, Protein: 8 grams, Carbohydrates: 46 grams, Fat: 12 grams, Saturated Fat: 2 grams, Cholesterol: 46 milligrams, Sodium: 320 milligrams, Fiber: 4 grams, and Sugar: 4 grams.

SHRIMP AND FETA ORZO SALAD

- Total Cooking Time: 20 minutes
- Prep Time: 10 minutes
- Servings: 4

Ingredients:

- 8 ounces orzo pasta
- 1 pound shrimp, peeled and deveined
- 1/2 cup crumbled feta cheese
- 1/4 cup sun-dried tomatoes, drained and chopped
- 1/4 cup of pitted and halved Kalamata olives
- 1/4 cup red onion, finely chopped
- 2 tablespoons fresh parsley, chopped
- 2 tablespoons extra virgin olive oil
- 1 tablespoon lemon juice
- Salt and pepper, to taste

Directions:

1. Prepare the orzo pasta as per the package instructions until it reaches al dente consistency. Then, drain and rinse it with cold water to cool.
2. In a large skillet, heat olive oil over medium heat. Cook the shrimp until they become pink and opaque, around 2-3 minutes per side. After cooking, remove the shrimp from the heat and let them cool.
3. In a sizable bowl, mix together the cooked orzo pasta, cooked shrimp, crumbled feta cheese, sun-dried tomatoes, Kalamata olives, red onion, and fresh parsley.
4. In a small bowl, whisk together the extra virgin olive oil, lemon juice, salt, and pepper.
5. Pour the dressing evenly over the orzo salad and delicately mix to thoroughly coat all the ingredients.
6. Taste and adjust the seasonings as desired.
7. Serve the shrimp and feta orzo salad chilled or at room temperature.

Nutritional breakdown per serving:

Calories: 380 kcal, Protein: 27 grams, Carbohydrates: 37 grams, Fat: 14 grams, Saturated Fat: 4 grams, Cholesterol: 180 milligrams, Sodium: 560 milligrams, Fiber: 3 grams, and Sugar: 3 grams.

STUFFED BELL PEPPERS WITH QUINOA AND FETA

- Total Cooking Time: 50 minutes
- Prep Time: 20 minutes
- Servings: 4

Ingredients:

- 4 bell peppers (any color)
- 1 cup cooked quinoa
- 1/2 cup crumbled feta cheese
- 1/4 cup sun-dried tomatoes, drained and chopped
- 1/4 cup of pitted and halved Kalamata olives
- 1/4 cup red onion, finely chopped
- 2 tablespoons fresh parsley, chopped
- 2 tablespoons extra virgin olive oil
- 1 tablespoon lemon juice
- 1 teaspoon dried oregano
- Salt and pepper, to taste

Directions:

1. Ensure that the oven has been preheated to 375°F (190°C) before you begin.
2. Remove the top portion of the bell peppers, eliminate the seeds and membranes, and then set them aside.
3. In a sizable bowl, mix together the cooked quinoa, crumbled feta cheese, sun-dried tomatoes, Kalamata olives, red onion, fresh parsley, extra virgin olive oil, lemon juice, dried oregano, salt, and pepper. Ensure the mixture is well combined.
4. Gently press the quinoa mixture into each bell pepper to firmly fill the pepper.
5. Arrange the filled bell peppers in a baking dish and then cover them with foil.
6. Cook in the oven that has been preheated for 30 minutes.
7. To uncover the dish and cook for an additional 10 minutes, or until the bell peppers have softened and developed a slight char.
8. Allow the dish to cool for a few minutes after removing it from the oven before serving.
9. Serve the stuffed bell peppers with quinoa and feta as a delicious and nutritious main dish or side.

Nutritional breakdown per serving:

Calories: 280 kcal, Protein: 10 grams, Carbohydrates: 30 grams, Fat: 14 grams, Saturated Fat: 4 grams, Cholesterol: 15 milligrams, Sodium: 480 milligrams, Fiber: 6 grams, and Sugar: 7 grams.

MEDITERRANEAN CHICKPEA SALAD

- Total Cooking Time: 15 minutes
- Prep Time: 10 minutes
- Servings: 4

Ingredients:

- 2 cans chickpeas, drained and rinsed
- 1 cucumber, diced
- 1 red bell pepper, diced
- 1/4 cup red onion, finely chopped
- 1/4 cup of pitted and halved Kalamata olives
- 1/4 cup crumbled feta cheese
- 2 tablespoons fresh parsley, chopped
- 2 tablespoons fresh lemon juice
- 2 tablespoons extra virgin olive oil
- 1 teaspoon dried oregano
- Salt and pepper, to taste

Directions:

1. In a spacious bowl, mix together the chickpeas, chopped cucumber, diced red bell pepper, finely chopped red onion, Kalamata olives, crumbled feta cheese, and fresh parsley.
2. Combine fresh lemon juice, extra virgin olive oil, dried oregano, salt, and pepper in a small bowl, stirring until all the ingredients are thoroughly mixed.
3. Gently pour the dressing over the chickpea salad and lightly toss to ensure an even coating of all the ingredients.
4. Taste and adjust the seasonings as desired.
5. Serve the Mediterranean chickpea salad chilled or at room temperature.

Nutritional breakdown per serving:

Calories: 280 kcal, Protein: 11 grams, Carbohydrates: 34 grams, Fat: 12 grams, Saturated Fat: 3 grams, Cholesterol: 8 milligrams, Sodium: 580 milligrams, Fiber: 9 grams, and Sugar: 6 grams.

GRILLED EGGPLANT AND HALLOUMI SANDWICH

- Total Cooking Time: 25 minutes
- Prep Time: 15 minutes
- Servings: 2

Ingredients:

- 1 medium eggplant, sliced into 1/2-inch rounds
- 8 ounces halloumi cheese, sliced
- 4 slices whole grain bread
- 2 tablespoons extra virgin olive oil
- 2 tablespoons balsamic vinegar
- 1 garlic clove, minced
- 1/4 teaspoon dried oregano
- Salt and pepper, to taste
- Fresh basil leaves, for garnish (optional)

Directions:

1. Before you start cooking, ensure that the grill or grill pan is preheated to medium heat.
2. In a small bowl, mix together the extra virgin olive oil, balsamic vinegar, minced garlic, dried oregano, salt, and pepper until thoroughly combined.
3. Apply the olive oil mixture to both sides of the eggplant slices and halloumi cheese slices, ensuring an even coating.
4. Place the eggplant slices and halloumi cheese slices on the grill. Cook for about 3-4 minutes per side, or until grill marks appear and the eggplant is tender.
5. Remove the grilled eggplant and halloumi from the grill and set aside.
6. Toast the slices of whole grain bread.
7. Assemble the sandwiches by layering the grilled eggplant and halloumi cheese between the slices of toasted bread.
8. If desired, garnish with fresh basil leaves.
9. Serve the grilled eggplant and halloumi sandwiches warm.

Nutritional breakdown per serving:

Calories: 450 kcal, Protein: 24 grams, Carbohydrates: 30 grams, Fat: 28 grams, Saturated Fat: 14 grams, Cholesterol: 60 milligrams, Sodium: 900 milligrams, Fiber: 7 grams, and Sugar: 8 grams.

LEMON GARLIC SHRIMP WITH ORZO

- Total Cooking Time: 25 minutes
- Prep Time: 10 minutes
- Servings: 4

Ingredients:

- 1 pound shrimp, peeled and deveined
- 8 ounces orzo pasta
- 4 cloves garlic, minced
- 2 tablespoons fresh lemon juice
- 2 tablespoons extra virgin olive oil
- 1 tablespoon chopped fresh parsley
- 1/2 teaspoon dried oregano
- Salt and pepper, to taste

Directions:

1. Cook the orzo pasta following the instructions on the package until it reaches the al dente stage. Then, drain the pasta and set it aside.
2. In a sizable skillet, heat the olive oil over medium heat, then add the minced garlic and sauté for about 1 minute until it releases its fragrance.
3. Place the shrimp into the skillet and cook for 2-3 minutes on each side until they turn pink and are thoroughly cooked.
4. Take the shrimp out of the skillet and place it to the side.
5. In the same skillet, add the cooked orzo pasta, lemon juice, chopped parsley, dried oregano, salt, and pepper. Stir well to combine and heat through for about 2 minutes.
6. Combine the cooked shrimp with the lemon garlic orzo mixture in the skillet, ensuring the shrimp is coated.
7. Continue cooking for another 1-2 minutes until everything is thoroughly heated.
8. Remove from heat and serve the lemon garlic shrimp with orzo immediately.

Nutritional breakdown per serving:

Calories: 320 kcal, Protein: 26 grams, Carbohydrates: 36 grams, Fat: 8 grams, Saturated Fat: 1 grams, Cholesterol: 215 milligrams, Sodium: 220 milligrams, Fiber: 2 grams, and Sugar: 1 grams.

TOMATO AND MOZZARELLA SALAD WITH BASIL PESTO

- Total Cooking Time: 15 minutes
- Prep Time: 10 minutes
- Servings: 4

Ingredients:

- 4 large tomatoes, sliced
- 8 ounces fresh mozzarella cheese, sliced
- 1/4 cup fresh basil leaves
- 2 tablespoons pine nuts
- 2 tablespoons grated Parmesan cheese
- 2 tablespoons extra virgin olive oil
- 1 clove garlic, minced
- Salt and pepper, to taste

Directions:

1. Place the tomato and mozzarella slices on a serving platter in an organized manner.

2. In a food processor or blender, mix together the fresh basil leaves, pine nuts, grated Parmesan cheese, minced garlic, extra virgin olive oil, salt, and pepper. Blend until smooth and well combined.

3. Pour the basil pesto over the tomato and mozzarella slices.

4. Serve the tomato and mozzarella salad with basil pesto immediately.

Nutritional breakdown per serving:

Calories: 250 kcal, Protein: 12 grams, Carbohydrates: 7 grams, Fat: 20 grams, Saturated Fat: 7 grams, Cholesterol: 30 milligrams, Sodium: 300 milligrams, Fiber: 2 grams, and Sugar: 4 grams.

GREEK SPINACH AND FETA PIE

- Total Cooking Time: 1 hour 15 minutes
- Prep Time: 30 minutes
- Servings: 6

Ingredients:

- 1 package frozen spinach, thawed and drained
- 1 cup crumbled feta cheese
- 1/2 cup ricotta cheese
- 1/4 cup grated Parmesan cheese
- 1/4 cup chopped fresh dill
- 1/4 cup chopped fresh parsley
- 3 green onions, finely chopped
- 2 cloves garlic, minced
- 4 eggs, beaten
- 1/4 teaspoon ground nutmeg
- Salt and pepper, to taste
- 8 sheets phyllo dough
- 1/4 cup unsalted butter, melted

Directions:

1. Warm up the oven to 375°F (190°C) before you begin.
2. In a large bowl, combine the thawed and drained spinach, crumbled feta cheese, ricotta cheese, grated Parmesan cheese, chopped fresh dill, chopped fresh parsley, finely chopped green onions, minced garlic, beaten eggs, ground nutmeg, salt, and pepper. Mix well.
3. On a spotless surface, lay down a sheet of phyllo dough and delicately apply some melted butter. Continue this step with three additional phyllo sheets, ensuring to brush each one with the melted butter.
4. Distribute the leftover spinach and cheese blend over the second tier of phyllo dough.
5. Layer four more sheets of phyllo dough on top of the spinach and cheese mixture, brushing each layer with melted butter.
6. Spread the remainder of the spinach and cheese mixture evenly over the second layer of phyllo dough.
7. Place the last four sheets of phyllo dough on the top, making sure to brush each layer with melted butter.
8. Trim any excess phyllo dough from the edges and tuck the edges into the pan.

9. Apply melted butter to the top layer of phyllo dough using a brush.
10. With a sharp knife, cut the top layer of phyllo dough into squares or triangles.
11. Place in the oven that has been preheated and bake for 45-50 minutes, or until the phyllo dough turns golden brown and becomes crispy.
12. Let the dish cool at room temperature for a few minutes before serving.
13. Serve the Greek spinach and feta pie warm or at room temperature.

Nutritional breakdown per serving:

Calories: 280 kcal, Protein: 12 grams, Carbohydrates: 18 grams, Fat: 18 grams, Saturated Fat: 10 grams, Cholesterol: 160 milligrams, Sodium: 570 milligrams, Fiber: 2 grams, and Sugar: 2 grams.

MEDITERRANEAN STUFFED ZUCCHINI BOATS

- Total Cooking Time: 45 minutes
- Prep Time: 20 minutes
- Servings: 4

Ingredients:

- 4 medium zucchini
- 1 tablespoon olive oil
- 1 small onion, finely chopped
- 2 cloves garlic, minced
- 1 red bell pepper, finely chopped
- 1 cup cherry tomatoes, halved
- 1/2 cup crumbled feta cheese
- 1/4 cup chopped fresh parsley
- 1/4 cup chopped fresh mint
- 1/4 teaspoon dried oregano
- Salt and pepper, to taste

Directions:

1. Before beginning the cooking process, preheat the oven to 375°F (190°C).
2. Cut each zucchini in half lengthwise. Scoop out the flesh from the center of each zucchini half, leaving about a 1/4-inch thick shell. Chop the scooped-out zucchini flesh and set aside.
3. Warm the olive oil in a spacious skillet over medium heat, then introduce the chopped onion and minced garlic, cooking until the onion achieves translucency.
4. Add the chopped zucchini flesh, red bell pepper, and cherry tomatoes to the skillet. Cook for about 5 minutes, until the vegetables are tender.
5. Take the skillet off the heat and stir in the crumbled feta cheese, chopped fresh parsley, chopped fresh mint, dried oregano, salt, and pepper.
6. Place the hollowed zucchini halves in a baking dish. Spoon the vegetable and feta mixture evenly into each zucchini boat.
7. Cover the baking dish using foil and place it in the preheated oven for 20-25 minutes, or until the zucchini reaches a soft and tender consistency.
8. Reveal the dish by removing the foil and proceed to bake for an additional 5 minutes to achieve a light browning on the tops.
9. Serve the Mediterranean stuffed zucchini boats hot.

Nutritional breakdown per serving:

Calories: 150 kcal, Protein: 7 grams, Carbohydrates: 14 grams, Fat: 8 grams, Saturated Fat: 3 grams, Cholesterol: 15 milligrams, Sodium: 220 milligrams, Fiber: 4 grams, and Sugar: 8 grams.

GRILLED LAMB KEBABS WITH YOGURT SAUCE

- Total Cooking Time: 30 minutes
- Prep Time: 15 minutes
- Servings: 4

Ingredients:

- 1 pound lamb, cut into 1-inch cubes
- 1/4 cup olive oil
- 2 tablespoons lemon juice
- 2 cloves garlic, minced
- 1 teaspoon dried oregano
- Salt and pepper, to taste
- 1 cup Greek yogurt
- 2 tablespoons fresh lemon juice
- 2 tablespoons chopped fresh mint
- 1 tablespoon chopped fresh dill
- 1 tablespoon chopped fresh parsley
- Salt and pepper, to taste

Directions:

1. Combine olive oil, lemon juice, minced garlic, dried oregano, salt, and pepper in a bowl. Toss the lamb cubes in the mixture for even coating, and then allow the lamb to marinate for a minimum of 10 minutes.
2. Preheat the grill to medium-high heat.
3. Preheat the grill to medium-high heat.
4. Thread the marinated lamb cubes onto skewers.
5. Grill the lamb kebabs for approximately 8-10 minutes, flipping them occasionally, until they reach your preferred level of doneness.
6. While the lamb is grilling, prepare the yogurt sauce. In a separate bowl, combine the Greek yogurt, fresh lemon juice, chopped fresh mint, chopped fresh dill, chopped fresh parsley, salt, and pepper. Mix well.
7. Remove the lamb kebabs from the grill and let them rest for a few minutes.
8. Serve the grilled lamb kebabs with the yogurt sauce on the side.

Nutritional breakdown per serving:

Calories: 350 kcal, Protein: 26 grams, Carbohydrates: 5 grams, Fat: 25 grams, Saturated Fat: 8 grams, Cholesterol: 85 milligrams, Sodium: 200 milligrams, Fiber: 1 grams, and Sugar: 3 grams.

CHAPTER 3
DINNER RECIPES

GREEK LEMON CHICKEN WITH ROASTED VEGETABLES

- Total Cooking Time: 1 hour 15 minutes
- Prep Time: 15 minutes
- Servings: 4

Ingredients:

- 4 boneless, skinless chicken breasts
- 4 tablespoons olive oil, divided
- 4 cloves garlic, minced
- Juice of 2 lemons
- 1 teaspoon dried oregano
- 1 teaspoon dried thyme
- 1 teaspoon dried rosemary
- Salt and pepper, to taste
- 1 pound baby potatoes, halved
- 2 bell peppers (red and yellow), sliced
- 1 red onion, sliced
- 1 cup cherry tomatoes
- Fresh parsley, for garnish

Directions:

1. Adjust the oven to a preheating temperature of 400 degrees Fahrenheit (200 degrees Celsius).
2. Blend 2 tablespoons of olive oil, minced garlic, lemon juice, dried oregano, dried thyme, dried rosemary, salt, and pepper in a small bowl to create a marinade.
3. To prepare the chicken breasts, place them in a shallow dish and make sure to coat them evenly with the marinade by pouring it over the top. Allow it to marinate for at least 15 minutes, or refrigerate overnight for more flavor.
4. In a large separate bowl, mix together the halved baby potatoes, bell peppers, red onion, cherry tomatoes, and the remaining 2 tablespoons of olive oil. Gently toss the vegetables with the oil and season with salt and pepper to ensure even coating.
5. Arrange the marinated chicken breasts and seasoned vegetables on a baking sheet, making sure they form a single layer and that the sheet is lined with either parchment paper or aluminum foil.

6. Put the ready dish in the preheated oven and bake for 30-35 minutes, remembering to stir the vegetables halfway through, until the chicken is thoroughly cooked and the vegetables are tender and have a light golden brown color.
7. Take the chicken out of the oven and allow it to rest for a few minutes before cutting into slices.
8. Serve the Greek lemon chicken with roasted vegetables hot, garnished with fresh parsley.
9. Enjoy this flavorful and wholesome Mediterranean-inspired meal!

Nutritional breakdown per serving:

Calories: 360 kcal, Protein: 34 grams, Carbohydrates: 26 grams, Fat: 14 grams, Saturated Fat: 2 grams, Cholesterol: 97 milligrams, Sodium: 115 milligrams, Fiber: 4 grams, and Sugar: 3 grams.

MEDITERRANEAN STUFFED BELL PEPPERS

- Total Cooking Time: 1 hour 15 minutes
- Prep Time: 20 minutes
- Servings: 4

Ingredients:

- 4 bell peppers with their tops removed and seeds taken out
- 1 cup cooked quinoa
- 1 cup canned chickpeas, rinsed and drained
- 1 cup diced tomatoes
- 1/2 cup chopped kalamata olives
- 1/2 cup crumbled feta cheese
- 2 tablespoons chopped fresh parsley
- 1 tablespoon lemon juice
- 2 tablespoons olive oil, divided
- Salt and pepper, to taste
- 1 zucchini, diced
- 1 yellow squash, diced
- 1 red onion, sliced
- 1 cup cherry tomatoes
- Fresh basil leaves, for garnish

Directions:

1. Before you begin, it's important to check that the oven has been preheated to 400 degrees Fahrenheit (200 degrees Celsius).
2. Position the bell peppers upright in a baking dish.
3. In a mixing bowl, blend together the cooked quinoa, chickpeas, diced tomatoes, kalamata olives, feta cheese, chopped parsley, lemon juice, 1 tablespoon of olive oil, salt, and pepper until thoroughly combined.
4. To prepare the bell peppers, evenly distribute the quinoa mixture inside each pepper.
5. Place the readied baking dish in the oven, ensure it is covered with foil, and let it bake for 30 minutes.
6. While the stuffed bell peppers are baking, prepare the roasted vegetables. In a separate baking dish, combine the diced zucchini, yellow squash, red onion, cherry tomatoes, remaining 1 tablespoon of olive oil, salt, and pepper. Toss to coat the vegetables.
7. After the stuffed bell peppers have baked for 30 minutes, remove the foil and place the baking dish with the roasted vegetables in the oven alongside the peppers.

8. Continue baking both the stuffed bell peppers and roasted vegetables for an additional 20-25 minutes, or until the bell peppers are tender and the vegetables are roasted to your liking.
9. Take out of the oven and allow it to cool for a short period.
10. Serve the Mediterranean stuffed bell peppers with roasted vegetables hot, garnished with fresh basil leaves.
11. Enjoy this delicious and wholesome Mediterranean-inspired meal!

Nutritional breakdown per serving:

Calories: 320 kcal, Protein: 11 grams, Carbohydrates: 15 grams, Fat: 14 grams, Saturated Fat: 4 grams, Cholesterol: 15 milligrams, Sodium: 480 milligrams, Fiber: 9 grams, and Sugar: 10 grams.

BAKED SALMON WITH GREEK SALAD

- Total Cooking Time: 30 minutes
- Prep Time: 10 minutes
- Servings: 4

Ingredients:

- 4 salmon fillets
- 2 tablespoons olive oil, divided
- 2 tablespoons lemon juice
- 2 cloves garlic, minced
- 1 teaspoon dried oregano
- Salt and pepper, to taste
- 2 cups cherry tomatoes, halved
- 1 cucumber, diced
- 1 red bell pepper, diced
- 1/2 red onion, thinly sliced
- 1/2 cup of Kalamata olives, pitless and sliced in half
- 4 ounces feta cheese, crumbled
- Fresh parsley, for garnish

Directions:

1. Adjust the oven to a preheating temperature of 400 degrees Fahrenheit (200 degrees Celsius).
2. You can start by setting the salmon fillets on a baking sheet that's been lined with either parchment paper or aluminum foil.
3. Blend 1 tablespoon of olive oil, lemon juice, minced garlic, dried oregano, salt, and pepper in a small bowl using a whisk.
4. Pour the marinade evenly onto the salmon fillets, ensuring they are completely covered.
5. Cook the salmon in the oven that has been preheated for 15-20 minutes, or until it easily flakes with a fork.
6. Sprinkle the remaining 1 tablespoon of olive oil over the salad and mix thoroughly.
7. Modify the seasoning with salt and pepper to align with your individual taste preferences.
8. Once the salmon is cooked, remove it from the oven and let it cool slightly.
9. Serve the baked salmon with a side of Greek salad, garnished with fresh parsley.
10. Enjoy this nutritious and flavorful Mediterranean-inspired meal!

Nutritional breakdown per serving:

Calories: 350 kcal, Protein: 32 grams, Carbohydrates: 10 grams, Fat: 20 grams, Saturated Fat: 5 grams, Cholesterol: 80 milligrams, Sodium: 450 milligrams, Fiber: 2 grams, and Sugar: 6 grams.

QUINOA TABBOULEH WITH GRILLED CHICKEN

- Total Cooking Time: 30 minutes
- Prep Time: 15 minutes
- Servings: 4

Ingredients:

- 1 cup quinoa
- 2 cups water
- 4 boneless, skinless chicken breasts
- 2 tablespoons olive oil, divided
- Juice of 1 lemon
- 2 cloves garlic, minced
- 1 cup cherry tomatoes, halved
- 1 cucumber, diced
- 1/2 red onion, finely chopped
- 1/2 cup chopped fresh parsley
- 1/4 cup chopped fresh mint
- Salt and pepper, to taste
- Lemon wedges, for serving

Directions:

1. Once you've rinsed the quinoa to eliminate any bitterness, bring the water to a boil, add the quinoa, and then let it simmer for approximately 15 minutes until it's tender and the water is fully absorbed. Remove from heat and allow to cool.
2. Preheat the grill to medium-high heat.
3. In a small bowl, whisk together 1 tablespoon of olive oil, lemon juice, minced garlic, salt, and pepper. Marinate the chicken breasts in the dish with the marinade, ensuring even coating, and let it sit for approximately 10 minutes.
4. Grill the chicken breasts for approximately 6-8 minutes on each side until they are thoroughly cooked and the internal temperature reaches 165°F (74°C). Take them off the grill and allow them to rest for a few minutes before slicing.
5. In a large bowl, combine the cooked quinoa, cherry tomatoes, cucumber, red onion, chopped parsley, chopped mint, and the remaining 1 tablespoon of olive oil. Toss to combine. Season with salt and pepper to taste.
6. Serve the quinoa tabbouleh with the grilled chicken and add lemon wedges for garnishing and squeezing over the dish.
7. Enjoy this refreshing and protein-packed Mediterranean-inspired meal!

Nutritional breakdown per serving:

Calories: 380 kcal, Protein: 34 grams, Carbohydrates: 35 grams, Fat: 12 grams, Saturated Fat: 2 grams, Cholesterol: 80 milligrams, Sodium: 120 milligrams, Fiber: 6 grams, and Sugar: 4 grams.

GRILLED SHRIMP SKEWERS WITH LEMON AND HERBS

- Total Cooking Time: 20 minutes
- Prep Time: 10 minutes
- Servings: 4

Ingredients:

- 1 pound large shrimp, peeled and deveined
- 2 tablespoons olive oil
- Juice of 1 lemon
- 2 cloves garlic, minced
- 1 teaspoon dried oregano
- 1 teaspoon dried thyme
- Salt and pepper, to taste
- Lemon wedges, for serving
- Fresh parsley, for garnish

Directions:

1. Preheat the grill to medium-high heat.
2. In a bowl, combine the olive oil, lemon juice, minced garlic, dried oregano, dried thyme, salt, and pepper. Mix well.
3. Combine the shrimp with the marinade in the bowl and toss to ensure they are coated. Allow the shrimp to marinate for approximately 5 minutes.
4. Thread the marinated shrimp onto skewers, making sure to leave a little space between each shrimp.
5. Grill the shrimp skewers on the preheated grill for roughly 2-3 minutes on each side, or until the shrimp become opaque and are cooked through.
6. Take the shrimp skewers off the grill and allow them to rest for a short while.
7. Serve the hot grilled shrimp skewers with a garnish of fresh parsley and accompanied by side lemon wedges.
8. Enjoy these flavorful and protein-rich Mediterranean-inspired shrimp skewers!

Nutritional breakdown per serving:

Calories: 150 kcal, Protein: 21 grams, Carbohydrates: 2 grams, Fat: 7 grams, Saturated Fat: 1 grams, Cholesterol: 170 milligrams, Sodium: 250 milligrams, Fiber: 0 grams, and Sugar: 0 grams.

RATATOUILLE WITH CHICKPEAS

- Total Cooking Time: 1 hour
- Prep Time: 15 minutes
- Servings: 4

Ingredients:

- 2 tablespoons olive oil
- 1 onion, diced
- 2 cloves garlic, minced
- 1 eggplant, diced
- 1 zucchini, diced
- 1 red bell pepper, diced
- 1 yellow bell pepper, diced
- 1 can (14 ounces) diced tomatoes
- 1 can (14 ounces) chickpeas, rinsed and drained
- 1 teaspoon dried thyme
- 1 teaspoon dried oregano
- Salt and pepper, to taste
- Fresh basil leaves, for garnish

Directions:

1. To avoid any mishaps, be mindful as you slowly heat the olive oil in a sizable pot or Dutch oven over medium heat, ensuring it does not become excessively hot.
2. Combine the finely chopped onion and minced garlic in the pot, sautéing until the onion becomes translucent and aromatic.
3. Add the diced eggplant, zucchini, red bell pepper, and yellow bell pepper to the pot. Sauté for about 5 minutes, or until the vegetables start to soften.
4. Stir in the diced tomatoes, chickpeas, dried thyme, dried oregano, salt, and pepper. Mix well to combine all the ingredients.
5. Lower the temperature to a gentle simmer, cover the pot, and allow the ratatouille to cook for roughly 45 minutes, stirring occasionally to avoid sticking.
6. After 45 minutes have passed, take off the cover and continue cooking for an additional 10-15 minutes until the vegetables have achieved the desired tenderness and the flavors have blended together.
7. Remove from heat and let the ratatouille cool slightly before serving.
8. Serve the ratatouille with chickpeas hot, garnished with fresh basil leaves.
9. Enjoy this hearty and flavorful Mediterranean-inspired dish!

Nutritional breakdown per serving:

Calories: 220 kcal, Protein: 8 grams, Carbohydrates: 35 grams, Fat: 7 grams, Saturated Fat: 1 grams, Cholesterol: 0 milligrams, Sodium: 350 milligrams, Fiber: 10 grams, and Sugar: 10 grams.

MEDITERRANEAN BAKED COD WITH TOMATOES AND OLIVES

- Total Cooking Time: 30 minutes
- Prep Time: 15 minutes
- Servings: 4

Ingredients:

- 4 cod fillets
- 2 tablespoons olive oil
- Juice of 1 lemon
- 2 cloves garlic, minced
- 1 teaspoon dried oregano
- 1 teaspoon dried basil
- Salt and pepper, to taste
- 1 cup cherry tomatoes, halved
- 1/2 cup of Kalamata olives, pitless and sliced in half
- Fresh parsley, for garnish

Directions:

1. To kick off the process, preheat the oven to 400°F (200°C).
2. Place the cod fillets neatly in the baking dish to prepare for cooking.
3. In a small bowl, whisk together the olive oil, lemon juice, minced garlic, dried oregano, dried basil, salt, and pepper.
4. Pour the marinade over the cod fillets, making sure they are evenly coated. Let them marinate for about 10 minutes.
5. Scatter the cherry tomatoes and Kalamata olives around the cod fillets in the baking dish.
6. Bake in the oven, preheated for 15-20 minutes, or until the cod is fully cooked and flakes easily with a fork.
7. Take out of the oven and allow it to cool for a bit.
8. Serve the Mediterranean baked cod hot, garnished with fresh parsley.
9. Enjoy this light and flavorful Mediterranean-inspired dish!

Nutritional breakdown per serving:

Calories: 220 kcal, Protein: 27 grams, Carbohydrates: 5 grams, Fat: 10 grams, Saturated Fat: 1.5 grams, Cholesterol: 55 milligrams, Sodium: 400 milligrams, Fiber: 1 grams, and Sugar: 2 grams.

LENTIL AND VEGETABLE MOUSSAKA

- Total Cooking Time: 1 hour 30 minutes
- Prep Time: 30 minutes
- Servings: 6

Ingredients:

- 1 tablespoon olive oil
- 1 onion, diced
- 2 cloves garlic, minced
- 1 eggplant, sliced into rounds
- 1 zucchini, sliced into rounds
- 1 red bell pepper, diced
- 1 yellow bell pepper, diced
- 1 cup cooked lentils
- 1 can (14 ounces) crushed tomatoes
- 2 tablespoons tomato paste
- 1 teaspoon dried oregano
- 1 teaspoon dried basil
- Salt and pepper, to taste
- 1 cup grated Parmesan cheese
- Fresh parsley, for garnish

Directions:

1. Adjust the oven to a preheating temperature of 400 degrees Fahrenheit (200 degrees Celsius).
2. Warm the olive oil in a generous-sized skillet over medium heat. Next, include the diced onion and minced garlic, and sauté until the onion turns translucent.
3. Add the sliced eggplant, zucchini, red bell pepper, and yellow bell pepper to the skillet. Cook for about 5 minutes, or until the vegetables start to soften.
4. Mix together the cooked lentils, crushed tomatoes, tomato paste, dried oregano, dried basil, salt, and pepper. Simmer the mixture for 10 minutes to encourage the flavors to meld together harmoniously.
5. In a baking dish that has been greased, create a layer using half of the vegetable and lentil mixture. Repeat the process by sprinkling half of the grated Parmesan cheese on top, followed by another layer of the remaining mixture and Parmesan cheese.
6. Position the preheated baking dish in the oven, cover it with foil, and let it bake for 40 minutes.

7. Proceed to bake the uncovered dish for an extra 10 minutes, or until the top becomes golden and bubbly.
8. Let the moussaka cool for a few minutes before serving. Garnish with fresh parsley.
9. Serve the Lentil and Vegetable Moussaka hot and enjoy!

Nutritional breakdown per serving:

Calories: 250 kcal, Protein: 12 grams, Carbohydrates: 35 grams, Fat: 8 grams, Saturated Fat: 3 grams, Cholesterol: 10 milligrams, Sodium: 400 milligrams, Fiber: 10 grams, and Sugar: 10 grams.

GREEK SPINACH AND FETA STUFFED CHICKEN BREAST

- Total Cooking Time: 40 minutes
- Prep Time: 15 minutes
- Servings: 4

Ingredients:

- 4 boneless, skinless chicken breasts
- 2 cups fresh spinach, chopped
- 1/2 cup crumbled feta cheese
- 1/4 cup sun-dried tomatoes, chopped
- 2 cloves garlic, minced
- 1 tablespoon olive oil
- 1 teaspoon dried oregano
- Salt and pepper, to taste
- Lemon wedges, for serving
- Fresh parsley, for garnish

Directions:

1. Adjust the oven to a preheating temperature of 400 degrees Fahrenheit (200 degrees Celsius).
2. In a bowl, combine the chopped spinach, crumbled feta cheese, sun-dried tomatoes, minced garlic, olive oil, dried oregano, salt, and pepper. Mix well to create the stuffing mixture.
3. Slice each chicken breast horizontally with a sharp knife to create a pocket for the stuffing. Be careful not to cut all the way through.
4. Fill each chicken breast with the spinach and feta mixture, distributing it evenly among the breasts.
5. Secure the openings of the chicken breasts with toothpicks to keep the stuffing in place.
6. Preheat a sizable oven-safe skillet over medium-high heat, then add a small amount of olive oil to the skillet.
7. Start by warming the skillet over medium heat, then add the stuffed chicken breasts. Cook for 3 to 4 minutes on each side until they acquire a golden brown color.
8. After the skillet has been preheated, it should be moved to the oven and the chicken should be baked for 20-25 minutes, or until it is fully cooked and reaches an internal temperature of 165°F (74°C).

9. After removing the skillet from the oven, it's best to let the chicken rest for a few minutes before serving.
10. Serve the Greek spinach and feta stuffed chicken breast hot, garnished with fresh parsley and lemon wedges on the side.
11. Enjoy this flavorful and protein-rich Mediterranean-inspired dish!

Nutritional breakdown per serving:

Calories: 280 kcal, Protein: 36 grams, Carbohydrates: 5 grams, Fat: 12 grams, Saturated Fat: 4 grams, Cholesterol: 100 milligrams, Sodium: 100 milligrams, Fiber: 1 grams, and Sugar: 2 grams.

MEDITERRANEAN GRILLED VEGETABLE WRAP

- Total Cooking Time: 30 minutes
- Prep Time: 15 minutes
- Servings: 4

Ingredients:

- 4 large whole wheat tortillas
- 1 zucchini, sliced lengthwise
- 1 yellow squash, sliced lengthwise
- 1 red bell pepper, seeded and quartered
- 1 red onion, sliced into rounds
- 1 cup cherry tomatoes, halved
- 1/4 cup of Kalamata olives, pitless and sliced in half
- 4 tablespoons hummus
- 2 tablespoons crumbled feta cheese
- Fresh basil leaves, for garnish
- Salt and pepper, to taste

Directions:

1. Before usage, ensure that the grill or grill pan is heated over medium-high heat.
2. Brush the zucchini, yellow squash, red bell pepper, and red onion with olive oil and season with salt and pepper.
3. Cook the vegetables on the grill for approximately 5-7 minutes per side, or until they achieve tenderness and develop grill marks.
4. Once grilling is complete, remove the vegetables from the heat and let them cool for a brief period.
5. Spread a border around the edges of each tortilla with 1 tablespoon of hummus.
6. Layer the grilled vegetables, cherry tomatoes, Kalamata olives, and crumbled feta cheese onto each tortilla.
7. Roll up the tortillas tightly, tucking in the sides as you go.
8. Slice each wrap in half diagonally and secure with toothpicks if needed.
9. Garnish with fresh basil leaves.
10. Serve the Mediterranean grilled vegetable wraps as a delicious and healthy meal.

Nutritional breakdown per serving:

Calories: 250 kcal, Protein: 9 grams, Carbohydrates: 38 grams, Fat: 8 grams, Saturated Fat: 2 grams, Cholesterol: 5 milligrams, Sodium: 500 milligrams, Fiber: 8 grams, and Sugar: 6 grams.

TUSCAN WHITE BEAN SOUP WITH KALE

- Total Cooking Time: 1 hour 30 minutes
- Prep Time: 15 minutes
- Servings: 6

Ingredients:

- 2 tablespoons olive oil
- 1 onion, diced
- 2 carrots, diced
- 2 celery stalks, diced
- 4 cloves garlic, minced
- 1 teaspoon dried thyme
- 1 teaspoon dried rosemary
- 1 bay leaf
- 4 cups vegetable broth
- 2 cans white beans, drained and rinsed
- 1 bunch of kale, with stems removed and leaves chopped
- Salt and pepper, to taste
- Grated Parmesan cheese, for serving (optional)

Directions:

1. When heating the olive oil in a large pot over medium heat, be sure to handle it with care. Next, add the diced onion, carrots, and celery, cooking until the vegetables have softened, usually about 5 minutes.
2. Add the minced garlic, dried thyme, dried rosemary, and bay leaf to the pot. Keep stirring and cooking for one more minute until the fragrance intensifies.
3. Transfer the vegetable broth into the pot and heat it until it reaches a boil. Following that, lower the heat to a gentle simmer and allow the soup to cook for 30 minutes, enabling the flavors to meld together perfectly.
4. Add the white beans and chopped kale to the pot. Mix thoroughly and let it simmer for an extra 10 minutes, or until the kale becomes wilted and tender.
5. Tailor the flavor of the soup to your liking by incorporating salt and pepper to fine-tune the seasoning based on your unique taste preferences.
6. Take out the bay leaf from the soup before serving.
7. Serve the Tuscan white bean soup in bowls and optionally add a sprinkle of grated Parmesan cheese on top.
8. Serve the soup hot and enjoy the comforting flavors of the Mediterranean!

Nutritional breakdown per serving:

Calories: 220 kcal, Protein: 10 grams, Carbohydrates: 34 grams, Fat: 6 grams, Saturated Fat: 1 grams, Cholesterol: 0 milligrams, Sodium: 600 milligrams, Fiber: 9 grams, and Sugar: 4 grams.

GREEK STYLE BAKED EGGPLANT WITH TOMATO SAUCE

- Total Cooking Time: 1 hour 15 minutes
- Prep Time: 30 minutes
- Servings: 4

Ingredients:

- 2 large eggplants
- 2 tablespoons olive oil
- 1 onion, diced
- 3 cloves garlic, minced
- 1 can (14 ounces) crushed tomatoes
- 1 teaspoon dried oregano
- 1 teaspoon dried basil
- Salt and pepper, to taste
- 1/2 cup crumbled feta cheese
- Fresh parsley, for garnish

Directions:

1. Adjust the oven to 375°F (190°C) and give it time to reach the desired temperature before use.
2. Slice the eggplants lengthwise into 1/2-inch thick slices. Spread the slices on a baking sheet, applying olive oil to both sides. Afterward, season with salt and pepper.
3. Roast the eggplant slices in the oven that has been preheated for 20-25 minutes, or until they are tender and have a slight golden hue.
4. While the eggplant is being cooked, warm up 1 tablespoon of olive oil in a skillet over medium heat. Subsequently, include the diced onion and minced garlic, and cook until the onion becomes translucent.
5. Stir in the crushed tomatoes, dried oregano, dried basil, salt, and pepper. Allow the tomato sauce to simmer for approximately 10 minutes, enabling the flavors to blend harmoniously.
6. After taking the eggplant slices out of the oven, allow them to cool for a short while.
7. In a baking dish coated with grease, place half of the eggplant slices in an even layer. Spread a portion of the tomato sauce over the eggplant.
8. Sprinkle half of the crumbled feta cheese on top. Repeat the process with an additional layer of the remaining eggplant slices, tomato sauce, and feta cheese.

91

9. Place the eggplant dish in the oven that has been preheated and bake for 20-25 minutes, or until the cheese has melted and is bubbling.
10. Remove from the oven and let it cool for a few minutes before serving.
11. Garnish with fresh parsley.
12. Serve the Greek style baked eggplant with tomato sauce as a delicious and healthy Mediterranean-inspired dish.

Nutritional breakdown per serving:

Calories: 180 kcal, Protein: 6 grams, Carbohydrates: 20 grams, Fat: 10 grams, Saturated Fat: 3 grams, Cholesterol: 15 milligrams, Sodium: 400 milligrams, Fiber: 8 grams, and Sugar: 10 grams.

LEMON HERB GRILLED PORK CHOPS WITH MEDITERRANEAN COUSCOUS

- Total Cooking Time: 30 minutes
- Prep Time: 15 minutes
- Servings: 4

Ingredients:

- 4 boneless pork chops
- 2 tablespoons olive oil
- 2 tablespoons lemon juice
- 2 cloves garlic, minced
- 1 teaspoon dried oregano
- 1 teaspoon dried thyme
- Salt and pepper, to taste
- 1 cup couscous
- 1 1/4 cups vegetable broth
- 1/4 cup chopped fresh parsley
- 1/4 cup chopped fresh mint
- 1/4 cup chopped Kalamata olives
- 1/4 cup crumbled feta cheese
- Lemon wedges, for serving

Directions:

1. Preheat the grill or grill pan at a medium-high temperature prior to usage.
2. In a small bowl, whisk together the olive oil, lemon juice, minced garlic, dried oregano, dried thyme, salt, and pepper to create a marinade.
3. While the pork chops are marinating, it's an opportune moment to prepare the couscous. Start by boiling the vegetable broth in a saucepan, then add the couscous, cover, remove from the heat, let it sit for 5 minutes, and gently fluff it with a fork.
4. While the pork chops are marinating, prepare the couscous. In a saucepan, gently heat the vegetable broth until it comes to a boil. Once boiling, stir in the couscous, cover the saucepan, and remove it from the heat. Allow it to sit for 5 minutes, then use a fork to fluff the couscous.
5. In a separate bowl, combine the cooked couscous, chopped parsley, chopped mint, chopped Kalamata olives, and crumbled feta cheese. Toss to combine.

6. Grill the marinated pork chops for approximately 4 to 5 minutes on each side, or until they achieve an internal temperature of 145°F (63°C). After grilling, remove the pork chops from the grill and let them rest for a few minutes before serving.
7. Pair the grilled pork chops with a serving of Mediterranean couscous and garnish with lemon wedges.
8. Enjoy this flavorful and satisfying Mediterranean-inspired meal!

Nutritional breakdown per serving:

Calories: 380 kcal, Protein: 30 grams, Carbohydrates: 27 grams, Fat: 16 grams, Saturated Fat: 5 grams, Cholesterol: 75 milligrams, Sodium: 550 milligrams, Fiber: 3 grams, and Sugar: 1 grams.

MOROCCAN SPICED CHICKPEA AND VEGETABLE TAGINE

- Total Cooking Time: 1 hour 15 minutes
- Prep Time: 30 minutes
- Servings: 4

Ingredients:

- 2 tablespoons olive oil
- 1 onion, diced
- 2 carrots, sliced
- 2 bell peppers (red and yellow), diced
- 2 cloves garlic, minced
- 1 teaspoon ground cumin
- 1 teaspoon ground coriander
- 1 teaspoon ground turmeric
- 1/2 teaspoon ground cinnamon
- 1 can (14 ounces) diced tomatoes
- 1 can (14 ounces) chickpeas, drained and rinsed
- 1 cup vegetable broth
- 1 cup diced butternut squash
- 1 cup chopped zucchini
- Salt and pepper, to taste
- Fresh cilantro, for garnish
- Cooked couscous, for serving

Directions:

1. In a large pot or tagine, heat the olive oil over medium heat. Add the diced onion, sliced carrots, and diced bell peppers. Cook the vegetables until they become tender, which usually takes around 5 minutes.
2. Cut each zucchini in half lengthwise. Use a spoon to remove the flesh, ensuring that a 1/4-inch thick shell remains. Reserve the scooped-out flesh for later use.
3. To get started, position the zucchini boats on a baking sheet that's been lined with parchment paper.
4. Add the diced butternut squash and chopped zucchini to the pot. Season with salt and pepper to taste.

5. After the mixture reaches a boiling point, decrease the heat to keep it at a gentle simmer. Cover the pot and allow the tagine to simmer for 45 minutes to facilitate the blending of flavors and the softening of the vegetables.
6. Remove the lid and give the tagine a stir. Adjust the seasoning if needed.
7. Serve the Moroccan spiced chickpea and vegetable tagine over cooked couscous.
8. Garnish with fresh cilantro.
9. Enjoy this aromatic and flavorful Mediterranean-inspired dish!

Nutritional breakdown per serving:

Calories: 280 kcal, Protein: 10 grams, Carbohydrates: 49 grams, Fat: 7 grams, Saturated Fat: 1 grams, Cholesterol: 0 milligrams, Sodium: 600 milligrams, Fiber: 12 grams, and Sugar: 10 grams.

MEDITERRANEAN STUFFED ZUCCHINI BOATS

- Total Cooking Time: 45 minutes
- Prep Time: 20 minutes
- Servings: 4

Ingredients:

- 4 medium zucchini
- 1 tablespoon olive oil
- 1 onion, diced
- 2 cloves garlic, minced
- 1 red bell pepper, diced
- 1 yellow bell pepper, diced
- 1 cup cherry tomatoes, halved
- 1 can (14 ounces) chickpeas, drained and rinsed
- 1 teaspoon dried oregano
- 1 teaspoon dried basil
- Salt and pepper, to taste
- 1/2 cup crumbled feta cheese
- Fresh parsley, for garnish

Directions:

1. Adjust the oven to a preheating temperature of 400 degrees Fahrenheit (200 degrees Celsius).
2. Split each zucchini in half lengthwise. Use a spoon to remove the inside, leaving about a 1/4-inch thick shell. Keep the scooped-out flesh for future use.
3. Position the zucchini boats on a baking sheet that has been covered with parchment paper.
4. First, you should heat the olive oil in a large pan over medium heat. Add the diced onion and minced garlic. Sauté until the onion becomes translucent.
5. Incorporate the diced red and yellow bell peppers into the ingredients in the skillet. Cook for about 5 minutes, or until the peppers are slightly softened.
6. Finely chop the zucchini flesh that was set aside and include it in the skillet. Stir in the cherry tomatoes, chickpeas, dried oregano, dried basil, salt, and pepper. Let the dish simmer for an extra 5 minutes to allow the flavors to meld together perfectly.
7. Spoon the vegetable mixture into the hollowed-out zucchini boats. Sprinkle the crumbled feta cheese on top.

8. To prepare the stuffed zucchini boats, position them in a preheated oven and cook for 20-25 minutes, or until the zucchini becomes tender and the cheese has melted and developed a golden hue.
9. Allow the dish to cool for a few minutes after removing it from the oven, and then it will be ready to serve.
10. Garnish with fresh parsley.
11. Serve the Mediterranean stuffed zucchini boats as a delightful and nutritious meal.

Nutritional breakdown per serving:

Calories: 180 kcal, Protein: 9 grams, Carbohydrates: 23 grams, Fat: 7 grams, Saturated Fat: 3 grams, Cholesterol: 15 milligrams, Sodium: 400 milligrams, Fiber: 7 grams, and Sugar: 9 grams.

HERB CRUSTED BAKED COD WITH MEDITERRANEAN QUINOA PILAF

- Total Cooking Time: 45 minutes
- Prep Time: 20 minutes
- Servings: 4

Ingredients:

- 4 cod fillets (about 6 ounces each)
- 2 tablespoons olive oil
- 2 tablespoons lemon juice
- 2 cloves garlic, minced
- 1 teaspoon dried thyme
- 1 teaspoon dried oregano
- Salt and pepper, to taste
- 1 cup quinoa
- 2 cups vegetable broth
- 1/4 cup chopped sun-dried tomatoes
- 1/4 cup chopped Kalamata olives
- 1/4 cup crumbled feta cheese
- Fresh parsley, for garnish

Directions:

1. Adjust the oven to a preheating temperature of 400 degrees Fahrenheit (200 degrees Celsius).
2. To heat the vegetable broth, place it in a saucepan and warm it until it reaches a boiling point. Once boiling, stir in the rinsed quinoa, reduce the heat to low, cover the saucepan, and let it simmer for approximately 15 minutes, or until the quinoa is fully cooked and the liquid is absorbed.
3. Place the cod fillets in the preheated oven and cook for 15-20 minutes, or until the fish becomes opaque and can be effortlessly flaked with a fork.
4. While the cod is baking, rinse the quinoa under cold water to remove any bitterness.
5. In a saucepan, bring the vegetable broth to a boil. Once boiling, stir in the rinsed quinoa, reduce the heat to low, cover the saucepan, and let it simmer for approximately 15 minutes, or until the quinoa is fully cooked and the liquid is absorbed.
6. Take the saucepan off the heat and allow it to sit, covered, for 5 minutes. Then, use a fork to fluff the quinoa.

7. Stir in the chopped sun-dried tomatoes, chopped Kalamata olives, and crumbled feta cheese into the cooked quinoa.
8. Serve the herb-crusted baked cod fillets over a bed of Mediterranean quinoa pilaf.
9. Garnish with fresh parsley.
10. Enjoy this delicious and nutritious Mediterranean-inspired meal!

Nutritional breakdown per serving:

Calories: 350 kcal, Protein: 30 grams, Carbohydrates: 32 grams, Fat: 12 grams, Saturated Fat: 3 grams, Cholesterol: 60 milligrams, Sodium: 600 milligrams, Fiber: 4 grams, and Sugar: 2 grams.

GREEK STYLE LAMB MEATBALLS WITH TZATZIKI SAUCE

- Total Cooking Time: 45 minutes
- Prep Time: 20 minutes
- Servings: 4

Ingredients:

For the Lamb Meatballs:

- 1 pound ground lamb
- 1/2 cup breadcrumbs
- 1/4 cup finely chopped red onion
- 2 cloves garlic, minced
- 2 tablespoons chopped fresh parsley
- 1 tablespoon chopped fresh mint
- 1 teaspoon dried oregano
- 1/2 teaspoon ground cumin
- Salt and pepper, to taste
- 1 tablespoon olive oil

For the Tzatziki Sauce:

- 1 cup Greek yogurt
- 1/2 cucumber, grated and wrung out to eliminate extra moisture
- 1 minced garlic clove
- 1 tablespoon lemon juice
- 1 tablespoon chopped fresh dill
- Salt and pepper, to taste

Directions:

1. To initiate, preheat the oven to 400 degrees Fahrenheit (200 degrees Celsius).
2. In a large bowl, combine the ground lamb, breadcrumbs, chopped red onion, minced garlic, chopped parsley, chopped mint, dried oregano, ground cumin, salt, and pepper. Stir thoroughly until the ingredients are uniformly combined.
3. Form the mixture into meatballs, each approximately 1-2 inches in diameter.

4. Begin by warming the olive oil in a skillet over medium heat until it attains the desired temperature. Next, introduce the lamb meatballs into the skillet and cook them for about 5 minutes, ensuring they are browned evenly on all sides.
5. Once the meatballs are browned, transfer them to a baking dish and then place the dish into the preheated oven. Cook for 15-20 minutes or until the meatballs are fully cooked and no longer pink in the center.
6. As the meatballs bake, get ready to prepare the tzatziki sauce. In a bowl, combine the Greek yogurt, grated cucumber, minced garlic, lemon juice, chopped dill, salt, and pepper. Mix well.
7. Serve the Greek style lamb meatballs with the tzatziki sauce on the side.
8. Enjoy these flavorful and juicy meatballs as a delicious Mediterranean-inspired meal!

Nutritional breakdown per serving:

Calories: 380 kcal, Protein: 27 grams, Carbohydrates: 12 grams, Fat: 25 grams, Saturated Fat: 10 grams, Cholesterol: 90 milligrams, Sodium: 300 milligrams, Fiber: 1 grams, and Sugar: 3 grams.

MEDITERRANEAN QUINOA SALAD WITH ROASTED VEGETABLES

- Total Cooking Time: 45 minutes
- Prep Time: 20 minutes
- Servings: 4

Ingredients:

- 1 cup quinoa
- 2 cups vegetable broth
- 1 red bell pepper, sliced
- 1 yellow bell pepper, sliced
- 1 zucchini, sliced
- 1 eggplant, diced
- 1 red onion, sliced
- 3 tablespoons olive oil
- 2 tablespoons lemon juice
- 2 cloves garlic, minced
- 1 teaspoon dried oregano
- Salt and pepper, to taste
- 1/4 cup chopped fresh parsley
- 1/4 cup crumbled feta cheese
- Lemon wedges, for serving

Directions:

1. Set the oven to a temperature of 400 degrees Fahrenheit (200 degrees Celsius) before use.
2. Rinse the quinoa under cold water to remove any bitterness.
3. In a saucepan, bring the vegetable broth to a boil, add the rinsed quinoa, and simmer for about 15 minutes until the quinoa is cooked and the liquid is absorbed. Then, remove from heat and let it cool.
4. Combine sliced red and yellow bell peppers, sliced zucchini, diced eggplant, and sliced red onion in a large baking dish. Drizzle olive oil, lemon juice, minced garlic, dried oregano, salt, and pepper, then toss to coat the vegetables evenly.
5. To achieve tenderness and a light caramelization, roast the vegetables in the preheated oven for 20-25 minutes. It's important to stir the vegetables halfway through the cooking process to ensure even browning.

6. Blend the cooked quinoa and roasted vegetables in a large bowl. Mix in chopped parsley and crumbled feta cheese, gently combining the ingredients.
7. Serve the Mediterranean quinoa salad with a squeeze of fresh lemon juice on top.
8. Enjoy this vibrant and nutritious Mediterranean-inspired salad!

Nutritional breakdown per serving:

Calories: 280 kcal, Protein: 9 grams, Carbohydrates: 36 grams, Fat: 12 grams, Saturated Fat: 3 grams, Cholesterol: 6 milligrams, Sodium: 400 milligrams, Fiber: 7 grams, and Sugar: 9 grams.

SHRIMP AND VEGETABLE STIR-FRY WITH BROWN RICE

- Total Cooking Time: 45 minutes
- Prep Time: 20 minutes
- Servings: 4

Ingredients:

- 1 cup brown rice
- 2 cups water
- 1 pound shrimp, peeled and deveined
- 2 tablespoons olive oil
- 2 cloves garlic, minced
- 1 red bell pepper, sliced
- 1 yellow bell pepper, sliced
- 1 zucchini, sliced
- 1 cup snap peas
- 1 cup broccoli florets
- 2 tablespoons low-sodium soy sauce
- 1 tablespoon honey
- 1 tablespoon lemon juice
- 1/2 teaspoon grated ginger
- Salt and pepper, to taste
- Fresh cilantro, for garnish

Directions:

1. Combine the brown rice and water in a saucepan. Simmer the mixture over low heat for around 40 minutes until the rice becomes tender and the water is fully absorbed. After taking it off the heat, let it sit covered for 5 minutes, then use a fork to fluff the rice.
2. Commence by heating the olive oil in a roomy skillet or wok over medium-high heat. Sauté the minced garlic for roughly 1 minute until it becomes aromatic.
3. To prepare the shrimp, put them in the skillet and cook for 2-3 minutes on each side until they attain a pink and opaque appearance. Then, take the shrimp out of the skillet and place them aside.

4. In the same skillet, place the sliced red and yellow bell peppers, sliced zucchini, snap peas, and broccoli florets. Stir-fry for about 5 minutes until the vegetables are crisp-tender.
5. In a small bowl, whisk together the low-sodium soy sauce, honey, lemon juice, grated ginger, salt, and pepper. Drizzle the sauce over the vegetables in the skillet and gently stir to ensure an even coating.
6. Place the cooked shrimp back into the skillet and mix with the vegetables and sauce. Continue cooking for an extra 2 minutes to ensure thorough heating.
7. Serve the shrimp and vegetable stir-fry over a bed of cooked brown rice.
8. Garnish with fresh cilantro.
9. Enjoy this delicious and nutritious Mediterranean-inspired meal!

Nutritional breakdown per serving:

Calories: 320 kcal, Protein: 24 grams, Carbohydrates: 38 grams, Fat: 9 grams, Saturated Fat: 1 grams, Cholesterol: 170 milligrams, Sodium: 600 milligrams, Fiber: 5 grams, and Sugar: 7 grams.

GREEK STYLE BAKED FALAFEL WITH TZATZIKI SAUCE

- Total Cooking Time: 45 minutes
- Prep Time: 20 minutes
- Servings: 4

Ingredients:

For the Falafel:

- 1 can chickpeas, drained and rinsed
- 1/2 cup chopped fresh parsley
- 1/4 cup chopped fresh cilantro
- 1/4 cup chopped red onion
- 2 cloves garlic, minced
- 1 teaspoon ground cumin
- 1 teaspoon ground coriander
- 1/2 teaspoon baking powder
- 2 tablespoons all-purpose flour
- Salt and pepper, to taste
- 2 tablespoons olive oil

For the Tzatziki Sauce:

- 1 cup Greek yogurt
- 1/2 cucumber and squeeze it to remove any extra moisture
- 1 clove garlic, minced
- 1 tablespoon lemon juice
- 1 tablespoon chopped fresh dill
- Salt and pepper, to taste

For Serving:

- Pita bread or lettuce leaves
- Sliced tomatoes
- Sliced cucumbers
- Sliced red onion

- Fresh parsley, for garnish

Directions:

1. Adjust the oven to 375°F (190°C) and give it time to reach the desired temperature before use.
2. In a food processor, combine the drained and rinsed chickpeas, chopped parsley, chopped cilantro, chopped red onion, minced garlic, ground cumin, ground coriander, baking powder, all-purpose flour, salt, and pepper. Pulse until the mixture is well combined and forms a coarse paste.
3. Shape the falafel mixture into small patties or balls, about 1-2 inches in diameter.
4. Meticulously warm the olive oil in a skillet over medium heat until it attains the necessary temperature. Add the falafel patties or balls and cook until golden brown on each side, about 2-3 minutes. You may need to cook them in batches.
5. Transfer the partially cooked falafel to a baking sheet lined with parchment paper. Place in the preheated oven for 15-20 minutes, or until the falafel is golden and thoroughly cooked.
6. While the falafel is baking, prepare the tzatziki sauce. In a bowl, combine the Greek yogurt, grated cucumber, minced garlic, lemon juice, chopped dill, salt, and pepper. Mix well.
7. Serve the baked falafel in pita bread or lettuce leaves. Top with sliced tomatoes, sliced cucumbers, sliced red onion, and a dollop of tzatziki sauce.
8. Garnish with fresh parsley.
9. Enjoy these flavorful and protein-packed Greek style falafel with refreshing tzatziki sauce!

Nutritional breakdown per serving:

Calories: 280 kcal, Protein: 12 grams, Carbohydrates: 36 grams, Fat: 10 grams, Saturated Fat: 2 grams, Cholesterol: 5 milligrams, Sodium: 400 milligrams, Fiber: 7 grams, and Sugar: 6 grams.

CHAPTER 4
DESSERT RECIPES

LEMON OLIVE OIL CAKE

- Total Cooking Time: 1 hour 15 minutes
- Prep Time: 15 minutes
- Servings: 8

Ingredients:

- 1 1/2 cups all-purpose flour
- 1/2 cup almond flour
- 1 1/2 teaspoons baking powder
- 1/2 teaspoon baking soda
- 1/4 teaspoon salt
- 3/4 cup granulated sugar
- Zest of 2 lemons
- 1/2 cup extra-virgin olive oil
- 3/4 cup unsweetened almond milk
- 1/4 cup freshly squeezed lemon juice
- 1 teaspoon vanilla extract
- Powdered sugar, for dusting (optional)

Directions:

1. To begin, start by setting the oven to 350°F (175°C) and allowing it to preheat. Get a 9-inch round cake pan ready by greasing it thoroughly and then dusting it with flour.
2. Combine the all-purpose flour, almond flour, baking powder, baking soda, and salt in a medium bowl using a whisk, and then set it aside to rest.
3. In a spacious mixing bowl, combine the granulated sugar and lemon zest, gently working the zest into the sugar with your fingers until its aroma is released.
4. Blend the olive oil, almond milk, lemon juice, and vanilla extract into the sugar and zest mixture, ensuring thorough combination using a whisk.
5. The process involves gently blending the dry ingredients with the wet mixture until just combined. It's crucial to avoid overmixing to prevent overworking the batter.
6. Carefully transfer the batter into the prepared cake pan and use a spatula to even out the top.
7. Bake the mixture in a preheated oven for 40 to 45 minutes, or until it is thoroughly cooked and a toothpick inserted into the center comes out clean.
8. Once the cake is removed from the oven and allowed to cool in the pan for 10 minutes, the subsequent step is to transfer it to a wire rack to ensure complete cooling. This process aids in ensuring that the cake cools evenly and maintains its texture.

9. After the cake has reached room temperature, you have the option to dust the top with powdered sugar.
10. Slice and serve the lemon olive oil cake. Enjoy!

Nutritional breakdown per serving:

Calories: 320 kcal, Protein: 4 grams, Carbohydrates: 36 grams, Fat: 18 grams, Saturated Fat: 2 grams, Cholesterol: 0 milligrams, Sodium: 230 milligrams, Fiber: 2 grams, and Sugar: 17 grams.

MEDITERRANEAN YOGURT PARFAIT WITH FRESH BERRIES AND HONEY

- Total Cooking Time: 10 minutes
- Prep Time: 5 minutes
- Servings: 2

Ingredients:

- 1 cup Greek yogurt
- 1 cup of assorted fresh berries, such as strawberries, blueberries, and raspberries
- 2 tablespoons honey
- 2 tablespoons chopped nuts (such as almonds, walnuts, or pistachios)
- Fresh mint leaves, for garnish (optional)

Directions:

1. In two serving glasses or bowls, evenly distribute half of the Greek yogurt at the bottom of each glass.
2. Add a layer of mixed fresh berries on top of the yogurt.
3. Drizzle 1 tablespoon of honey over each layer of berries.
4. Continue the layering process with an additional layer of Greek yogurt, fresh berries, and another drizzle of honey.
5. Sprinkle the chopped nuts on top of each parfait.
6. Garnish with fresh mint leaves, if desired.
7. Serve immediately and enjoy the refreshing Greek Yogurt Parfait with Fresh Berries and Honey.

Nutritional breakdown per serving:

Calories: 220 kcal, Protein: 14 grams, Carbohydrates: 32 grams, Fat: 6 grams, Saturated Fat: 1 grams, Cholesterol: 10 milligrams, Sodium: 65 milligrams, Fiber: 4 grams, and Sugar: 26 grams.

ALMOND AND ORANGE BLOSSOM COOKIES

- Total Cooking Time: 25 minutes
- Prep Time: 15 minutes
- Servings: 12-15 cookies

Ingredients:

- 1 cup almond flour
- 1/2 cup unsalted almond butter
- 1/4 cup honey
- 1 tablespoon orange blossom water
- 1/2 teaspoon vanilla extract
- 1/4 teaspoon almond extract
- Zest of 1 orange
- 1/4 teaspoon salt
- 1/4 cup sliced almonds, for topping (optional)

Directions:

1. Start by ensuring that the oven is preheated to 350°F (175°C) before beginning the cooking process.
2. In a medium mixing bowl, combine the almond flour, almond butter, honey, orange blossom water, vanilla extract, almond extract, orange zest, and salt. Mix until all the ingredients are well combined and form a dough.
3. Mold the dough into small balls with a 1-inch diameter and position them on the baking sheet that has been prepared. Apply a gentle touch to each ball to softly press it down and flatten it.
4. For additional flavor, consider placing a few sliced almonds on top of each cookie and gently pressing them into the dough.
5. Put the cookies in the oven that has been preheated and bake for 10-12 minutes, or until the edges develop a golden brown hue.
6. After taking the cookies out of the oven, it's best to let them cool on the baking sheet for a brief period before moving them to a wire rack for thorough cooling.
7. Once cooled, store the Almond and Orange Blossom Cookies in an airtight container.

Nutritional breakdown per serving (1 cookie):

Calories: 120 kcal, Protein: 4 grams, Carbohydrates: 8 grams, Fat: 9 grams, Saturated Fat: 1 grams, Cholesterol: 0 milligrams, Sodium: 30 milligrams, Fiber: 2 grams, and Sugar: 4 grams.

FIG AND WALNUT TART

- Total Cooking Time: 1 hour 15 minutes
- Prep Time: 30 minutes
- Servings: 8

Ingredients:

For the crust:

- 1 1/2 cups all-purpose flour
- 1/3 cup powdered sugar
- 1/4 teaspoon salt
- 1/2 cup cold, cubed unsalted butter
- 1 large egg yolk
- 2 tablespoons ice water

For the filling:

- 1 cup chopped walnuts
- 1/4 cup honey
- 1/4 cup unsalted butter, melted
- 1/4 cup light brown sugar
- 1 teaspoon vanilla extract
- 1/2 teaspoon ground cinnamon
- 6-8 fresh figs, stemmed and sliced

For the glaze:

- 1/4 cup apricot preserves
- 1 tablespoon water

Directions:

1. Get ready for baking by preheating the oven to 375°F (190°C) and applying butter or oil to a 9-inch tart pan with a removable bottom.
2. Combine the all-purpose flour, powdered sugar, and salt in a food processor. Afterward, add the cold cubed butter and pulse until the mixture achieves a texture resembling coarse crumbs.

3. Combine the egg yolk with ice water in a small bowl and stir until fully blended. Gradually combine the egg mixture with the ingredients in the food processor while pulsing until the dough becomes a unified mixture.
4. Place the dough on a surface that has been lightly dusted with flour and form it into a disk shape. Wrap the dough using plastic wrap and refrigerate it for 30 minutes.
5. Roll out the cold dough on a floured surface until it is the appropriate size for the tart pan. Press the dough into the pan, ensuring an even layer on the bottom and sides. Trim any excess dough.
6. In a medium bowl, mix together the chopped walnuts, honey, melted butter, brown sugar, vanilla extract, and cinnamon until well combined.
7. Spread the walnut mixture evenly onto the bottom of the prepared tart crust.
8. Arrange the sliced figs on top of the walnut mixture, pressing them gently into the filling.
9. Bake in the preheated oven for 35-40 minutes, or until the crust is golden brown and the filling is set.
10. In a small saucepan, gently warm the apricot preserves and water over low heat until they melt into a liquid state. Then, spread the glaze over the top of the tart while it is still warm.
11. After the tart has cooled completely, it's ready to be served. Slice it and savor each delicious bite!

Nutritional breakdown per serving:

Calories: 380 kcal, Protein: 5 grams, Carbohydrates: 42 grams, Fat: 23 grams, Saturated Fat: 8 grams, Cholesterol: 55 milligrams, Sodium: 100 milligrams, Fiber: 3 grams, and Sugar: 24 grams.

PISTACHIO BAKLAVA

- Total Cooking Time: 1 hour 30 minutes
- Prep Time: 45 minutes
- Servings: 12-15 pieces

Ingredients:

- 1 cup shelled pistachios, finely chopped
- 1/2 cup unsalted butter, melted
- 1/4 cup granulated sugar
- 1 teaspoon ground cinnamon
- 1/2 teaspoon ground cardamom
- 1/2 teaspoon vanilla extract
- 1/2 cup honey
- 1 package (16 ounces) phyllo dough, thawed

Directions:

1. Before you continue, make sure to preheat the oven to 350°F (175°C) and apply a layer of grease to a 9x13-inch baking dish.
2. In a bowl, combine the finely chopped pistachios, granulated sugar, ground cinnamon, ground cardamom, and vanilla extract. Mix well and set aside.
3. Unfold the phyllo dough and place a moistened cloth over it to keep it from drying out.
4. Place one sheet of phyllo dough in the prepared baking dish. Brush it with melted butter.
5. Repeat step 4 using 5-6 additional sheets of phyllo dough, and brush each layer with melted butter.
6. Sprinkle a generous amount of the pistachio mixture evenly over the phyllo dough.
7. Continue layering the phyllo dough and pistachio mixture, brushing each layer with melted butter, until all the pistachio mixture is used.
8. Place an additional 5-6 sheets of phyllo dough on top of the baklava, and brush each layer with melted butter.
9. Slice the baklava into diamond or square shapes with a sharp knife.
10. Place in the oven that has been preheated and bake for 30-35 minutes, or until it turns golden brown and crispy.
11. While the baklava is baking, heat the honey in a small saucepan over low heat until warm.
12. After the baklava has finished baking, take it out of the oven and promptly drizzle the warm honey over it, making sure to cover all the pieces.

13. Once the baklava is done baking, let it cool down entirely in the baking dish before serving. This step is essential for the syrup to fully soak into the layers.
14. Serve the Pistachio Baklava at room temperature and enjoy!

Nutritional breakdown per serving (1 piece):

Calories: 250 kcal, Protein: 3 grams, Carbohydrates: 20 grams, Fat: 15 grams, Saturated Fat: 5 grams, Cholesterol: 20 milligrams, Sodium: 90 milligrams, Fiber: 2 grams, and Sugar: 14 grams.

ROASTED APRICOTS WITH HONEY AND THYME

- Total Cooking Time: 25 minutes
- Prep Time: 10 minutes
- Servings: 4

Ingredients:

- 8 ripe apricots, halved and pitted
- 2 tablespoons honey
- 1 tablespoon fresh thyme leaves
- Greek yogurt, for serving (optional)

Directions:

1. Begin the process by preheating the oven to 400°F (200°C), then proceed to line the baking sheet with parchment paper.
2. Place the apricot halves, cut side up, on the prepared baking sheet.
3. Drizzle the honey over the apricots, ensuring each half is coated.
4. To achieve a slight caramelized texture, bake the apricots in the preheated oven for 15-20 minutes until they have softened.
5. Bake the apricots in the preheated oven for 15-20 minutes until they have softened and acquired a gentle caramelized texture.
6. Remove from the oven and let the roasted apricots cool for a few minutes.
7. Consider serving the roasted apricots as they are, or with a dollop of Greek yogurt if you'd like.
8. Enjoy the delicious Roasted Apricots with Honey and Thyme!

Nutritional breakdown per serving:

Calories: 80 kcal, Protein: 1 grams, Carbohydrates: 0 grams, Fat: 0.5 grams, Saturated Fat: 0 grams, Cholesterol: 0 milligrams, Sodium: 0 milligrams, Fiber: 2 grams, and Sugar: 1 grams.

GREEK YOGURT PANNA COTTA WITH RASPBERRY SAUCE

- Total Cooking Time: 4 hours 30 minutes (including chilling time)
- Prep Time: 30 minutes
- Servings: 4

Ingredients:

For the Panna Cotta:

- 2 cups Greek yogurt
- 1 cup whole milk
- 1/4 cup honey
- 1 teaspoon vanilla extract
- 2 teaspoons gelatin powder
- 2 tablespoons cold water

For the Raspberry Sauce:

- 2 cups fresh or frozen raspberries
- 2 tablespoons honey
- 1 tablespoon lemon juice

Optional Garnish:

- Fresh mint leaves

Directions:

1. Evenly distribute the gelatin powder across the surface of the cold water in a small bowl and allow it to rest for 5 minutes to become hydrated.
2. In a saucepan, heat the milk over medium heat until it starts to steam. Do not let it boil.
3. Mix the Greek yogurt, honey, and vanilla extract in a different bowl and stir until thoroughly combined.
4. Gradually incorporate the warm milk into the yogurt mixture, ensuring a continuous whisking motion to prevent the formation of lumps.
5. Move the mixture back to the saucepan and warm it over low heat, stirring continuously, until it gently simmers.
6. Take the saucepan off the heat and incorporate the bloomed gelatin. Stir until the gelatin is fully dissolved.

7. Let the mixture cool for 10 minutes, then transfer it into individual serving glasses or ramekins.
8. Place the glasses in the refrigerator and let them chill for at least 4 hours, or until the panna cotta is set.

For the Raspberry Sauce:

1. Blend together the raspberries, honey, and lemon juice in a small saucepan.
2. To heat gently over medium heat, stirring occasionally, until the raspberries become soft and the sauce thickens slightly (approximately 5-7 minutes).
3. After removing from the heat, allow the sauce to cool down to room temperature.
4. Once cooled, strain the sauce through a fine-mesh sieve to remove the seeds.

To Serve:

1. To take out the chilled panna cotta from the fridge.
2. Spoon the raspberry sauce over each panna cotta.
3. Garnish with fresh mint leaves, if desired.
4. Serve the Greek Yogurt Panna Cotta with Raspberry Sauce chilled and enjoy!

Nutritional breakdown per serving:

Calories: 250 kcal, Protein: 14 grams, Carbohydrates: 32 grams, Fat: 8 grams, Saturated Fat: 5 grams, Cholesterol: 25 milligrams, Sodium: 70 milligrams, Fiber: 2 grams, and Sugar: 14 grams.

OLIVE OIL AND ORANGE CAKE

- Total Cooking Time: 1 hour 30 minutes
- Prep Time: 30 minutes
- Servings: 8-10

Ingredients:

- 1 1/2 cups all-purpose flour
- 1 1/2 teaspoons baking powder
- 1/2 teaspoon baking soda
- 1/4 teaspoon salt
- 3 large eggs
- 1 cup granulated sugar
- 1/2 cup extra-virgin olive oil
- 1/2 cup freshly squeezed orange juice
- Zest of 1 orange
- 1 teaspoon vanilla extract

For the Orange Syrup:

- 1/4 cup freshly squeezed orange juice
- 1/4 cup granulated sugar

For the Orange Glaze:

- 1 cup powdered sugar
- 2 tablespoons freshly squeezed orange juice

Optional Garnish:

- Orange slices
- Fresh mint leaves

Directions:

1. To begin, heat the oven to 350°F (175°C) and get a 9-inch round cake pan ready. To prepare the pan, coat it with grease and then lay parchment paper on the bottom.
2. Once the flour, baking powder, baking soda, and salt have been combined in a medium bowl, set the mixture aside for later use.

3. To combine the eggs and granulated sugar in a spacious bowl, whisk until the mixture achieves a lighter color and a fluffy texture.
4. Gradually incorporate the olive oil while continuously whisking the mixture.
5. Add the orange juice, orange zest, and vanilla extract. Mix until well combined.
6. Delicately integrate the dry ingredients into the wet mixture, stirring until they are only just combined, taking care not to overmix.
7. Carefully transfer the batter into the ready cake pan and use a spatula to even out the top.
8. Place in an oven that has been preheated for 30-35 minutes, or until a toothpick inserted into the center emerges clean.
9. During the cake's baking time, get the orange syrup ready. Gently heat the orange juice and granulated sugar in a small saucepan over medium heat until the sugar dissolves, and then set the mixture aside.
10. After the cake has completed baking, take it out of the oven and allow it to cool in the pan for 10 minutes.
11. Gently flip the cake onto a wire rack, take off the parchment paper, and place the cake back on the wire rack.
12. With a toothpick or skewer, make holes all over the top of the cake.
13. Gently drizzle the orange syrup over the cake, enabling it to seep into the openings and soak up the syrup.
14. Allow the cake to cool entirely on the wire rack.

For the Orange Glaze:

1. Mix together the powdered sugar and freshly squeezed orange juice in a small bowl, stirring until the mixture reaches a smooth and thoroughly blended consistency.
2. Apply the glaze to the cooled cake, allowing it to cascade down the sides.
3. Add orange slices and fresh mint leaves as a garnish, if preferred.
4. Serve the Olive Oil and Orange Cake at room temperature and enjoy!

Nutritional breakdown per serving:

Calories (1 slice): 280 kcal, Protein: 4 grams, Carbohydrates: 56 grams, Fat: 12 grams, Saturated Fat: 2 grams, Cholesterol: 56 milligrams, Sodium: 190 milligrams, Fiber: 1 grams, and Sugar: 4 grams.

ALMOND BUTTER ENERGY BALLS

- Total Cooking Time: 15 minutes
- Prep Time: 10 minutes
- Servings: 12-15 energy balls

Ingredients:

- 1 cup rolled oats
- 1/2 cup almond butter
- 1/4 cup honey or maple syrup
- 1/4 cup chopped almonds
- 1/4 cup dried cranberries or raisins
- 1 tablespoon chia seeds
- 1 teaspoon vanilla extract
- Pinch of salt
- Optional: shredded coconut or cocoa powder for coating

Directions:

1. In a large mixing bowl, combine the rolled oats, almond butter, honey or maple syrup, chopped almonds, dried cranberries or raisins, chia seeds, vanilla extract, and a pinch of salt.
2. Mix all the ingredients until they are completely incorporated. The mixture should be sticky and hold together when pressed.
3. Take about a tablespoon of the mixture and roll it between your palms to form a ball. Repeat with the remaining mixture.
4. If you'd like, you can opt to coat the energy balls with shredded coconut or cocoa powder to provide an additional layer of flavor.
5. After arranging the energy balls on a baking sheet or plate, refrigerate them for a minimum of 30 minutes to assist in the setting process.
6. Once chilled, the Almond Butter Energy Balls are ready to be enjoyed! Keep them in a sealed container in the fridge for a maximum of seven days.

Nutritional breakdown per serving:

Calories (1 energy ball): 120 kcal, Protein: 3 grams, Carbohydrates: 12 grams, Fat: 7 grams, Saturated Fat: 1 grams, Cholesterol: 0 milligrams, Sodium: 20 milligrams, Fiber: 2 grams, and Sugar: 5 grams.

CHOCOLATE DIPPED MEDJOOL DATES WITH SEA SALT

- Total Cooking Time: 15 minutes
- Prep Time: 10 minutes
- Servings: 12-15 dates

Ingredients:

- 12-15 Medjool dates, pitted
- 4 ounces dark chocolate, chopped
- Sea salt, for sprinkling

Directions:

1. Place parchment paper on the baking sheet.
2. Heat the dark chocolate in a microwave-safe bowl, stirring at 30-second intervals until it becomes smooth and fully melted.
3. Dip each pitted Medjool date into the melted chocolate, coating it halfway. Allow any excess chocolate to drip off.
4. Place the chocolate-dipped dates on the prepared baking sheet.
5. Sprinkle a bit of sea salt onto every date coated in chocolate.
6. Refrigerate the dates for about 10 minutes, or until the chocolate is set.
7. Once the chocolate is set, the Chocolate Dipped Medjool Dates with Sea Salt are ready to be enjoyed!
8. Place any remaining portions in a sealed container and store them in the refrigerator for a maximum of one week.

Nutritional breakdown per serving:

Calories (1 date): 80 kcal, Protein: 1 grams, Carbohydrates: 16 grams, Fat: 2 grams, Saturated Fat: 1 grams, Cholesterol: 16 milligrams, Sodium: 10 milligrams, Fiber: 2 grams, and Sugar: 14 grams.

WATERMELON AND FETA SALAD WITH MINT

- Total Cooking Time: 15 minutes
- Prep Time: 10 minutes
- Servings: 4

Ingredients:

- 4 cups cubed watermelon
- 1 cup crumbled feta cheese
- 1/4 cup fresh mint leaves, torn
- 2 tablespoons extra-virgin olive oil
- 1 tablespoon fresh lime juice
- Salt and pepper, to taste

Directions:

1. Combine the diced watermelon, crumbled feta cheese, and torn mint leaves in a sizable mixing bowl.
2. Mix together the extra-virgin olive oil and fresh lime juice in a small bowl, ensuring they are thoroughly blended using a whisk.
3. Drizzle the olive oil and lime juice mixture over the watermelon, feta, and mint.
4. Gently combine the salad, making sure the dressing evenly coats all the ingredients.
5. Modify the seasoning by adding salt and pepper to suit your personal taste.
6. Serve the Watermelon and Feta Salad with Mint immediately and enjoy!

Nutritional breakdown per serving:

Calories: 160 kcal, Protein: 5 grams, Carbohydrates: 13 grams, Fat: 11 grams, Saturated Fat: 5 grams, Cholesterol: 25 milligrams, Sodium: 330 milligrams, Fiber: 1 grams, and Sugar: 10 grams.

STRAWBERRY GREEK YOGURT FROZEN POPS

- Total Cooking Time: 4 hours 30 minutes (including freezing time)
- Prep Time: 10 minutes
- Servings: 6 popsicles

Ingredients:

- 2 cups fresh strawberries, hulled and chopped
- 1 cup Greek yogurt
- 2 tablespoons honey or maple syrup
- 1 teaspoon vanilla extract

Directions:

1. Mix the fresh strawberries, Greek yogurt, honey or maple syrup, and vanilla extract together using a blender or food processor.
2. Blend until smooth and well combined.
3. Fill the popsicle molds with the mixture, ensuring to leave some space at the top to allow for expansion.
4. Insert popsicle sticks into each mold.
5. Chill the popsicle molds in the freezer for a minimum of 4 hours, or until they are fully frozen.

To Serve:

1. Take out the frozen popsicles from the molds by briefly rinsing them under warm water.
2. Serve the Strawberry Greek Yogurt Frozen Pops immediately and enjoy!

Nutritional breakdown per serving (1 popsicle):

Calories: 70 kcal, Protein: 4 grams, Carbohydrates: 2 grams, Fat: 0.5 grams, Saturated Fat: 0 grams, Cholesterol: 2 milligrams, Sodium: 20 milligrams, Fiber: 1 grams, and Sugar: 11 grams.

HONEY ROASTED FIGS WITH GREEK YOGURT

- Total Cooking Time: 20 minutes
- Prep Time: 10 minutes
- Servings: 4

Ingredients:

- 8 fresh figs, halved
- 2 tablespoons honey
- 1 tablespoon extra-virgin olive oil
- 1/2 teaspoon ground cinnamon
- Greek yogurt, for serving
- Optional toppings: chopped nuts, mint leaves

Directions:

1. Adjust the oven to a temperature of 400°F (200°C) for preheating.
2. In a small bowl, whisk together the honey, olive oil, and ground cinnamon.
3. Arrange the fig halves on a baking sheet, with the cut side facing upward.
4. Drizzle the honey mixture over the figs, making sure to coat them evenly.
5. Roast the figs in the preheated oven for about 10 minutes, or until they are soft and caramelized.
6. Take out the figs from the oven and allow them to cool for a short time.
7. Serve the Honey Roasted Figs with a dollop of Greek yogurt.
8. Optional: Sprinkle chopped nuts and mint leaves over the top for added flavor and garnish.

Nutritional breakdown per serving:

Calories: 120 kcal, Protein: 1 grams, Carbohydrates: 23 grams, Fat: 4 grams, Saturated Fat: 0.5 grams, Cholesterol: 0 milligrams, Sodium: 0 milligrams, Fiber: 3 grams, and Sugar: 20 grams.

GREEK YOGURT CHEESECAKE WITH BERRY COMPOTE

- Total Cooking Time: 4 hours 30 minutes (including chilling time)
- Prep Time: 30 minutes
- Servings: 8

Ingredients:

For the Crust:

- 1 1/2 cups graham cracker crumbs
- 1/4 cup melted butter
- 2 tablespoons honey

For the Filling:

- 2 cups Greek yogurt
- 8 ounces cream cheese, softened
- 1/2 cup honey
- 2 teaspoons vanilla extract
- Zest of 1 lemon

For the Berry Compote:

- 2 cups mixed berries (such as strawberries, blueberries, and raspberries)
- 2 tablespoons honey
- 1 tablespoon lemon juice

Directions:

1. Blend the graham cracker crumbs, melted butter, and honey in a medium bowl, making sure the crumbs are evenly coated to create the crust.
2. Gently apply even pressure to the crust mixture in the bottom of a 9-inch springform pan, using a spoon or a flat-bottomed glass to ensure a thorough and uniform press.
3. Combine the softened cream cheese, Greek yogurt, honey, vanilla extract, and lemon zest in a large mixing bowl to create the filling mixture. Beat until smooth and well combined.
4. Carefully drizzle the filling mixture over the crust in the springform pan. Smooth the top with a spatula.

5. Place the cheesecake in the refrigerator and let it chill for at least 4 hours, or until set.
6. In a small saucepan, combine the mixed berries, honey, and lemon juice for the berry compote. Let the mixture gently simmer over medium heat for about 5 minutes or until the berries have softened and released their juices, ensuring to stir occasionally.
7. Take the cheesecake out of the refrigerator and delicately detach the sides of the springform pan.
8. Serve the Greek Yogurt Cheesecake with a spoonful of the berry compote on top of each slice.

Nutritional breakdown per serving:

Calories: 350 kcal, Protein: 9 grams, Carbohydrates: 39 grams, Fat: 18 grams, Saturated Fat: 10 grams, Cholesterol: 55 milligrams, Sodium: 250 milligrams, Fiber: 2 grams, and Sugar: 28 grams.

ALMOND FLOUR CHOCOLATE CHIP COOKIES

- Total Cooking Time: 25 minutes
- Prep Time: 15 minutes
- Servings: 12 cookies

Ingredients:

- 1 1/2 cups almond flour
- 1/4 cup coconut flour
- 1/2 teaspoon baking soda
- 1/4 teaspoon salt
- 1/4 cup coconut oil, melted
- 1/4 cup honey or maple syrup
- 1 teaspoon vanilla extract
- 1/2 cup dark chocolate chips

Directions:

1. Prepare the oven for baking by preheating it to 350°F (175°C), and then cover a baking sheet with parchment paper.
2. In a medium bowl, whisk together the almond flour, coconut flour, baking soda, and salt.
3. In a separate bowl, blend the melted coconut oil with honey or maple syrup and vanilla extract until thoroughly combined.
4. Combine the moist components with the dry components and mix until thoroughly blended.
5. Fold in the dark chocolate chips.
6. Employ a cookie scoop or a tablespoon to divide the dough onto the arranged baking sheet, ensuring that they are spaced apart.
7. Try using the back of a spoon or your fingertips to gently flatten each cookie.
8. Place the mixture in the oven and bake it for 10 to 12 minutes, or until the edges develop a golden brown color.
9. After taking the cookies out of the oven, it's best to let them cool on the baking sheet for a short period before moving them to a wire rack for thorough cooling.

Nutritional breakdown per serving (1 cookie):

Calories: 150 kcal, Protein: 3 grams, Carbohydrates: 12 grams, Fat: 11 grams, Saturated Fat: 5 grams, Cholesterol: 0 milligrams, Sodium: 100 milligrams, Fiber: 2 grams, and Sugar: 8 grams.

ORANGE AND ALMOND SEMOLINA CAKE

- Total Cooking Time: 1 hour 30 minutes
- Prep Time: 20 minutes
- Servings: 8

Ingredients:

For the Cake:

- 1 cup almond flour
- 1 cup semolina flour
- 1 teaspoon baking powder
- 1/4 teaspoon salt
- 3/4 cup sugar
- 3 large eggs
- 1/2 cup Greek yogurt
- 1/4 cup olive oil
- Zest of 1 orange
- Juice of 1 orange

For the Syrup:

- 1/2 cup fresh orange juice
- 1/4 cup honey
- Zest of 1 orange

For Garnish:

- Sliced almonds
- Fresh orange slices

Directions:

1. Before getting started, preheat the oven to 350°F (175°C) and apply a layer of grease to a 9-inch round cake pan.
2. In a medium bowl, whisk together the almond flour, semolina flour, baking powder, and salt.
3. Combine the sugar and eggs in a different large bowl to achieve a light and fluffy texture.
4. Mix the Greek yogurt, olive oil, orange zest, and orange juice with the egg mixture. Stir well until thoroughly combined.

5. Combine the dry components with the wet components little by little, stirring until the batter is uniform and well mixed.
6. After pouring the batter into the prepped cake pan, use a spatula to make sure the top is even.
7. Put it in the oven that has been preheated and bake for 30-35 minutes, or until a toothpick inserted into the center emerges clean.
8. While the cake is in the oven, make the syrup Mix the orange juice, honey, and orange zest in a small saucepan. Gently heat the mixture over medium heat until it reaches a simmer. Then, remove from the heat and set it aside.
9. After the cake is baked, take it out of the oven and allow it to cool in the pan for 10 minutes.
10. Delicately move the cake onto a serving dish. With a toothpick or skewer, make several punctures all over the cake.
11. Carefully drizzle the syrup over the cake, letting it soak into the punctures and coat the entire surface.
12. Let the cake cool completely before serving.
13. Garnish with sliced almonds and fresh orange slices, if desired.
14. Slice and serve the Orange and Almond Semolina Cake. Enjoy!

Nutritional breakdown per serving:

Calories: 320 kcal, Protein: 7 grams, Carbohydrates: 42 grams, Fat: 15 grams, Saturated Fat: 2 grams, Cholesterol: 70 milligrams, Sodium: 120 milligrams, Fiber: 2 grams, and Sugar: 24 grams.

BAKED PEARS WITH HONEY AND CINNAMON

- Total Cooking Time: 40 minutes
- Prep Time: 10 minutes
- Servings: 4

Ingredients:

- 4 ripe pears
- 2 tablespoons honey
- 1 teaspoon ground cinnamon
- Optional toppings: Greek yogurt, chopped nuts, dried fruits

Directions:

1. Start by warming the oven to 375°F (190°C) and lining a baking dish with parchment paper.
2. Cut the pears in half lengthwise and remove the cores.
3. Place the pear halves cut side up in the baking dish.
4. Drizzle the honey over the pears, making sure to coat them evenly.
5. Sprinkle the ground cinnamon over the pears.
6. Bake in the oven that has been preheated for 25-30 minutes, or until the pears are soft and caramelized.
7. Remove from the oven and let the baked pears cool slightly.
8. Serve the Baked Pears with a dollop of Greek yogurt and sprinkle with chopped nuts or dried fruits, if desired.

Nutritional breakdown per serving:

Calories (1 pear half): 90 kcal, Protein: 1 grams, Carbohydrates: 24 grams, Fat: 0 grams, Saturated Fat: 0 grams, Cholesterol: 0 milligrams, Sodium: 0 milligrams, Fiber: 4 grams, and Sugar: 17 grams.

GREEK YOGURT CHOCOLATE MOUSSE

- Total Cooking Time: 2 hours 30 minutes (including chilling time)
- Prep Time: 20 minutes
- Servings: 4

Ingredients:

- 1 cup Greek yogurt
- 1/4 cup cocoa powder
- 1/4 cup honey or maple syrup
- 1 teaspoon vanilla extract
- Pinch of salt
- Optional toppings: fresh berries, chopped nuts, grated dark chocolate

Directions:

1. Combine Greek yogurt, cocoa powder, honey or maple syrup, vanilla extract, and salt in a medium bowl until the mixture is smooth and well blended.
2. Divide the mixture into serving glasses or bowls.
3. Cover the glasses or bowls with plastic wrap and place them in the refrigerator for a minimum of 2 hours, or until the mousse has solidified.
4. Once the mousse is set, remove from the refrigerator.
5. Garnish with fresh berries, chopped nuts, or grated dark chocolate, if desired.
6. Serve the Greek Yogurt Chocolate Mousse chilled and enjoy!

Nutritional breakdown per serving:

Calories: 120 kcal, Protein: 7 grams, Carbohydrates: 22 grams, Fat: 2 grams, Saturated Fat: 1 grams, Cholesterol: 5 milligrams, Sodium: 40 milligrams, Fiber: 2 grams, and Sugar: 17 grams.

HONEY AND LEMON RICOTTA TART

- Total Cooking Time: 1 hour 30 minutes
- Prep Time: 30 minutes
- Servings: 8

Ingredients:

For the Crust:

- 1 1/2 cups graham cracker crumbs
- 1/4 cup melted butter
- 2 tablespoons honey

For the Filling:

- 2 cups ricotta cheese
- 1/2 cup honey
- Zest of 1 lemon
- Juice of 1 lemon
- 1 teaspoon vanilla extract

For Garnish:

- Lemon slices
- Fresh mint leaves

Directions:

1. Commence by preheating the oven to 350°F (175°C) and then lightly coating a 9-inch tart pan with a thin layer of grease.
2. To make the crust, mix together the graham cracker crumbs, melted butter, and honey in a medium bowl until the crumbs are thoroughly coated.
3. Gently apply consistent pressure as you mold the mixture into the bottom and sides of the tart pan, forming the crust. Use the back of a spoon or a flat-bottomed glass to press it down firmly.
4. Bake the prepared crust in the preheated oven for 10 minutes. Remove from the oven and let it cool completely.
5. In a sizable mixing bowl, blend the ricotta cheese, honey, lemon zest, lemon juice, and vanilla extract for the filling. Mix until thoroughly combined and smooth.
6. Pour the filling into the cooled crust, ensuring an even distribution.

7. Place the tart in the refrigerator and let it chill for at least 1 hour, or until set.
8. Once the tart is set, remove it from the refrigerator.
9. Spruce up with lemon slices and fresh mint leaves.
10. Slice and serve the Honey and Lemon Ricotta Tart. Enjoy!

Nutritional breakdown per serving:

Calories: 320 kcal, Protein: 8 grams, Carbohydrates: 40 grams, Fat: 15 grams, Saturated Fat: 9 grams, Cholesterol: 55 milligrams, Sodium: 200 milligrams, Fiber: 1 grams, and Sugar: 30 grams.

WALNUT AND HONEY PHYLLO ROLLS

- Total Cooking Time: 40 minutes
- Prep Time: 20 minutes
- Servings: 12 rolls

Ingredients:

- 1/2 cup walnuts, finely chopped
- 1/4 cup honey
- 1/2 teaspoon ground cinnamon
- 1/4 teaspoon ground nutmeg
- 12 sheets phyllo dough
- 1/4 cup melted butter

Directions:

1. Prepare the baking sheet by placing parchment paper on it and then preheat the oven to 350°F (175°C).
2. In a small bowl, mix together the chopped walnuts, honey, ground cinnamon, and ground nutmeg until well combined.
3. Place a single sheet of phyllo dough on a clean surface and lightly brush it with melted butter.
4. Place an additional sheet of phyllo dough on the top and also brush it with melted butter. Continue this procedure until you have a stack of 4 phyllo sheets.
5. Spoon a portion of the walnut and honey mixture along the shorter edge of the phyllo stack, leaving a small border.
6. Roll the phyllo stack tightly, starting from the edge with the walnut mixture, to form a log.
7. Repeat steps 3-6 with the remaining phyllo sheets and walnut mixture to make a total of 12 rolls.
8. Arrange the rolls on the lined baking sheet and use melted butter to brush the tops.
9. Bake the rolls in the preheated oven for 15 to 20 minutes, or until they become golden brown and crispy.
10. Remove from the oven and let the phyllo rolls cool slightly before serving.

Nutritional breakdown per serving (1 roll):

Calories: 120 kcal, Protein: 2 grams, Carbohydrates: 15 grams, Fat: 6 grams, Saturated Fat: 2 grams, Cholesterol: 5 milligrams, Sodium: 75 milligrams, Fiber: 1 grams, and Sugar: 5 grams.

CHAPTER 5
SNACK RECIPES

AVOCADO AND HUMMUS TOAST

- Total Cooking Time: 10 minutes
- Prep Time: 5 minutes
- Servings: 2

Ingredients:

- 2 slices whole grain bread
- 1 ripe avocado
- 4 tablespoons hummus
- 1 small tomato, sliced
- Fresh basil leaves, for garnish
- Salt and pepper, to taste

Directions:

1. Toast the slices of whole grain bread to your desired level of crispness.
2. While the bread is toasting, cut the ripe avocado in half, remove the pit, and scoop the flesh into a bowl. Gently use a fork to crush the avocado until it attains a smooth and even texture.
3. After the bread has been toasted, apply 2 tablespoons of hummus to each slice.
4. Evenly distribute the mashed avocado on top of the layer of hummus.
5. Place the sliced tomato on top of the avocado.
6. Modify the flavor with salt and pepper to match your individual preference.
7. Garnish with fresh basil leaves.
8. Serve the avocado and hummus toast immediately.

Nutritional breakdown per serving:

Calories: 250 kcal, Protein: 8 grams, Carbohydrates: 30 grams, Fat: 12 grams, Saturated Fat: 2 grams, Cholesterol: 0 milligrams, Sodium: 350 milligrams, Fiber: 8 grams, and Sugar: 3 grams.

ENERGY BALLS (VARIETY OF FLAVORS)

- Total Cooking Time: 15 minutes
- Prep Time: 10 minutes
- Servings: 12-15 energy balls (depending on size)

Ingredients:

- 1 cup dates, pitted
- 1 cup of assorted nuts, like almonds, cashews, or walnuts
- 2 tablespoons of a nut-based spread, such as peanut butter or almond butter
- 2 tablespoons cocoa powder
- 2 tablespoons shredded coconut
- Optional flavor variations: crushed dried fruits, chia seeds, matcha powder, vanilla extract, etc.

Directions:

1. Utilize a food processor to blend the dates and nuts until they amalgamate into a cohesive, adhesive mixture.
2. Add the nut butter, cocoa powder, shredded coconut, and any optional flavor variations. Process until well combined.
3. The mixture should be sticky enough to hold together when pressed. If it's too dry, add a little more nut butter or a splash of water.
4. Form small portions of the mixture into spherical shapes by gently rolling them with your hands.
5. Arrange the energy balls on a baking sheet that has been lined with parchment paper.
6. Repeat until all the mixture is used.
7. If desired, coat the energy balls with extra shredded coconut or cocoa powder to enhance their flavor and texture.
8. Chill the energy balls in the refrigerator for a minimum of 30 minutes to allow them to solidify.
9. Place the prepared mixture in a sealed container and store it in the fridge for a maximum of two weeks.

Nutritional breakdown per serving (1 energy ball):

Calories: 100 kcal, Protein: 2 grams, Carbohydrates: 12 grams, Fat: 5 grams, Saturated Fat: 1 grams, Cholesterol: 0 milligrams, Sodium: 5 milligrams, Fiber: 2 grams, and Sugar: 9 grams.

ROASTED CHICKPEAS (SEASONED WITH SPICES)

- Total Cooking Time: 40 minutes
- Prep Time: 5 minutes
- Servings: 4

Ingredients:

- 2 cans chickpeas, drained and rinsed
- 2 tablespoons olive oil
- 1 teaspoon paprika
- 1/2 teaspoon cumin
- 1/2 teaspoon chili powder
- Salt and pepper, to taste

Directions:

1. Before commencing the baking process, it is important to ensure that the oven has been preheated to 400°F (200°C).
2. After rinsing and draining the chickpeas, use a paper towel to pat them dry.
3. Blend the chickpeas with olive oil, paprika, cumin, chili powder, salt, and pepper in a bowl, ensuring even coverage.
4. Ensure the seasoned chickpeas are arranged in a single layer on a baking sheet.
5. Bake the chickpeas in the oven at the preheated temperature for 30-35 minutes, or until they turn crispy and attain a golden brown color.
6. Agitate the chickpeas every 10 minutes to promote uniform cooking.
7. After taking them out of the oven, allow them to cool for a bit before serving.
8. Enjoy the roasted chickpeas as a crunchy and flavorful snack.

Nutritional breakdown per serving:

Calories: 180 kcal, Protein: 8 grams, Carbohydrates: 25 grams, Fat: 6 grams, Saturated Fat: 1 grams, Cholesterol: 0 milligrams, Sodium: 350 milligrams, Fiber: 7 grams, and Sugar: 4 grams.

GUACAMOLE AND VEGGIE STICKS

- Total Cooking Time: 10 minutes
- Prep Time: 10 minutes
- Servings: 4

Ingredients:

- 2 ripe avocados
- 1 small red onion, finely chopped
- 1 tomato, diced
- 1 jalapeño pepper, seeded and minced
- 2 tablespoons lime juice
- 2 tablespoons chopped fresh cilantro
- Salt and pepper, to taste
- Assorted veggies for dipping (carrot sticks, celery sticks, bell pepper strips, cucumber slices, cherry tomatoes, etc.)

Directions:

1. In a bowl, use a fork to create a smooth texture by mashing the avocados until they reach the desired consistency.
2. Stir in the chopped red onion, diced tomato, minced jalapeño pepper, lime juice, chopped cilantro, salt, and pepper. Mix well to combine all the ingredients.
3. Adjust the seasoning according to taste.
4. Wash and cut the vegetables into sticks or slices.
5. Arrange the veggie sticks on a platter.
6. Serve the guacamole alongside the veggie sticks for dipping.

Nutritional breakdown per serving:

Calories: 150 kcal, Protein: 3 grams, Carbohydrates: 12 grams, Fat: 12 grams, Saturated Fat: 2 grams, Cholesterol: 0 milligrams, Sodium: 10 milligrams, Fiber: 7 grams, and Sugar: 2 grams.

CUCUMBER SUSHI ROLLS WITH AVOCADO AND CARROT

- Total Cooking Time: 20 minutes
- Prep Time: 15 minutes
- Servings: 4

Ingredients:

- 2 large cucumbers
- 1 ripe avocado, thinly sliced
- 1 carrot, julienned
- 2 tablespoons rice vinegar
- 1 tablespoon soy sauce
- 1 teaspoon sesame oil
- Optional toppings: sesame seeds, nori strips, pickled ginger, wasabi

Directions:

1. Employ a vegetable peeler or mandoline slicer to strip the cucumbers and slice them lengthwise into thin strips.
2. Lay the cucumber strips flat on a clean surface.
3. Place a few avocado slices and carrot juliennes at one end of each cucumber strip.
4. Gently roll up the cucumber strip, starting from the end with the filling, until you reach the other end. Secure with a toothpick if needed.
5. Repeat the process with the remaining cucumber strips and filling ingredients.
6. In a small bowl, whisk together the rice vinegar, soy sauce, and sesame oil to make a dipping sauce.
7. Serve the cucumber sushi rolls with the dipping sauce on the side.
8. Optional: Sprinkle sesame seeds on top of the rolls and garnish with nori strips, pickled ginger, or wasabi for added flavor and presentation.

Nutritional breakdown per serving:

Calories: 70 kcal, Protein: 2 grams, Carbohydrates: 6 grams, Fat: 5 grams, Saturated Fat: 1 grams, Cholesterol: 0 milligrams, Sodium: 200 milligrams, Fiber: 3 grams, and Sugar: 2 grams.

VEGAN NACHOS WITH CASHEW CHEESE AND BLACK BEANS

- Total Cooking Time: 25 minutes
- Prep Time: 15 minutes
- Servings: 4

Ingredients:

- Tortilla chips
- 1 cup cashews, soaked in water for 2-4 hours
- 1/4 cup nutritional yeast
- 1 tablespoon lemon juice
- 1/2 teaspoon garlic powder
- 1/2 teaspoon onion powder
- Salt, to taste
- 1 cup cooked black beans
- 1 carrot, grated
- Optional toppings: diced tomatoes, sliced jalapeños, chopped cilantro, sliced black olives, guacamole, salsa, etc.

Directions:

1. Before beginning the baking process, it is important to adjust the oven temperature to 350°F (175°C).
2. Drain and rinse the soaked cashews.
3. In a blender or food processor, combine the cashews, nutritional yeast, lemon juice, garlic powder, onion powder, and salt. Blend until smooth and creamy. To reach the desired consistency, consider adding a small amount of water if necessary.
4. Arrange a layer of tortilla chips in a baking dish.
5. Spoon the cashew cheese over the chips, covering them evenly.
6. Sprinkle the cooked black beans and grated carrot over the cheese.
7. Feel free to include your preferred toppings, such as diced tomatoes, sliced jalapeños, chopped cilantro, or sliced black olives.
8. Put the nachos in the oven that has been preheated and bake for approximately 10 minutes, or until the cheese becomes warm and bubbly.
9. Take the item out of the oven and allow it to cool for a short time.
10. Serve the vegan nachos with your favorite dips, such as guacamole or salsa.

Nutritional breakdown per serving:

Calories: 250 kcal, Protein: 8 grams, Carbohydrates: 30 grams, Fat: 12 grams, Saturated Fat: 2 grams, Cholesterol: 0 milligrams, Sodium: 200 milligrams, Fiber: 6 grams, and Sugar: 2 grams.

ZUCCHINI FRITTERS WITH TZATZIKI SAUCE

- Total Cooking Time: 30 minutes
- Prep Time: 15 minutes
- Servings: 4

Ingredients:

For the Zucchini Fritters:

- 2 medium zucchinis, grated
- 1/2 teaspoon salt
- 1/4 cup of chickpea flour or all-purpose flour
- 2 tablespoons nutritional yeast
- 1/2 teaspoon garlic powder
- 1/2 teaspoon onion powder
- 1/4 teaspoon ground black pepper
- 2 tablespoons chopped fresh parsley
- 2 tablespoons olive oil (for frying)

For the Vegan Tzatziki Sauce:

- 1 cup dairy-free yogurt
- 1/2 cucumber and press out the excess water
- 1 clove garlic, minced
- 1 tablespoon lemon juice
- 1 tablespoon chopped fresh dill
- Salt and pepper, to taste

Directions:

1. Transfer the grated zucchini to a colander, sprinkle it with salt, and let it sit for around 10 minutes to draw out excess moisture.
2. Extract as much liquid as you can from the grated zucchini by squeezing it.
3. In a mixing bowl, combine the grated zucchini, chickpea flour, nutritional yeast, garlic powder, onion powder, black pepper, and chopped parsley. Make sure to blend the ingredients thoroughly until they are uniformly incorporated.
4. Initiate the process by gradually heating the olive oil in a broad frying pan over medium heat until it attains the preferred temperature.

5. Take a small handful of the zucchini mixture and shape it into a fritter. Place it in the skillet and flatten it slightly with a spatula. Repeat with the remaining mixture, leaving some space between each fritter.
6. Cook the fritters for about 3-4 minutes on each side, or until they are golden brown and crispy.
7. To remove any excess oil, place the fritters from the pan onto a plate that has been lined with paper towels.
8. In a small bowl, combine the dairy-free yogurt, grated cucumber, minced garlic, lemon juice, chopped dill, salt, and pepper. Mix well to make the vegan tzatziki sauce.
9. Serve the zucchini fritters warm with a side of vegan tzatziki sauce.

Nutritional breakdown per serving:

Calories: 180 kcal, Protein: 8 grams, Carbohydrates: 20 grams, Fat: 9 grams, Saturated Fat: 1 grams, Cholesterol: 0 milligrams, Sodium: 400 milligrams, Fiber: 4 grams, and Sugar: 6 grams.

CARROT AND BEETROOT HUMMUS WITH WHOLE GRAIN CRACKERS

- Total Cooking Time: 20 minutes
- Prep Time: 15 minutes
- Servings: 4

Ingredients:

For the Carrot and Beetroot Hummus:

- 1 cup cooked chickpeas
- 1 medium carrot, peeled and chopped
- 1 small beetroot, peeled and chopped
- 2 tablespoons tahini
- 2 tablespoons lemon juice
- 1 clove garlic, minced
- 2 tablespoons olive oil
- 1/2 teaspoon ground cumin
- Salt and pepper, to taste

For the Whole Grain Crackers:

- 1 cup whole wheat flour
- 1/4 cup ground flaxseed
- 1/4 cup sesame seeds
- 1/4 teaspoon salt
- 1/4 teaspoon baking powder
- 1/4 cup olive oil
- 1/4 cup water

Directions:

For the Carrot and Beetroot Hummus:

1. Combine the cooked chickpeas, diced carrot, and beetroot in a food processor. Add the tahini, lemon juice, minced garlic, olive oil, ground cumin, salt, and pepper, and blend until the mixture reaches a smooth and well-combined consistency.
2. To achieve a smooth and creamy consistency, continue processing while occasionally scraping down the sides.

3. Consider sampling the dish and adjusting the seasoning as necessary.
4. Move the hummus into a serving bowl and keep it aside for future use.

For the Whole Grain Crackers:

1. Begin by adjusting the oven temperature to 350°F (175°C) and allowing it to preheat.
2. Combine the whole wheat flour, ground flaxseed, sesame seeds, salt, and baking powder in a mixing bowl, ensuring they are thoroughly blended until well combined.
3. Add the olive oil and water to the dry ingredients. Mix until a dough forms.
4. Roll the dough out onto a surface that has been dusted with flour, ensuring it reaches a thickness of around 1/8 inch.
5. Cut the dough into desired cracker shapes using a knife or cookie cutter.
6. Arrange the crackers on a baking sheet that has been lined with parchment paper.
7. Bake in the oven that has been preheated for 10-12 minutes, or until the crackers become golden brown and crispy.
8. Take them out of the oven and allow them to cool down entirely.
9. Serve the Carrot and Beetroot Hummus with the Whole Grain Crackers.

Nutritional breakdown per serving:

Calories: 220 kcal, Protein: 7 grams, Carbohydrates: 23 grams, Fat: 12 grams, Saturated Fat: 2 grams, Cholesterol: 0 milligrams, Sodium: 250 milligrams, Fiber: 6 grams, and Sugar: 3 grams.

VEGAN CAPRESE SKEWERS WITH CHERRY TOMATOES, BASIL, AND VEGAN MOZZARELLA

- Total Cooking Time: 15 minutes
- Prep Time: 10 minutes
- Servings: 4

Ingredients:

- 1 pint cherry tomatoes
- 1 bunch fresh basil leaves
- 8 ounces vegan mozzarella cheese, cut into bite-sized pieces
- Balsamic glaze, for drizzling
- Salt and pepper, to taste
- Bamboo skewers

Directions:

1. After washing the cherry tomatoes, gently dry them by patting with a paper towel.
2. Take a bamboo skewer and thread one cherry tomato onto it, followed by a basil leaf, and then a piece of vegan mozzarella. Continue following this pattern until the skewer is completely filled.
3. Carry on with the process using the remaining ingredients.
4. Arrange the caprese skewers on a serving platter.
5. Drizzle balsamic glaze over the skewers.
6. Season with salt and pepper to match your individual flavor preferences.

Nutritional breakdown per serving:

Calories: 120 kcal, Protein: 8 grams, Carbohydrates: 10 grams, Fat: 6 grams, Saturated Fat: 1 grams, Cholesterol: 0 milligrams, Sodium: 200 milligrams, Fiber: 2 grams, and Sugar: 6 grams.

ROASTED EDAMAME BEANS WITH SEA SALT AND CHILI FLAKES

- Total Cooking Time: 25 minutes
- Prep Time: 10 minutes
- Servings: 4

Ingredients:

- 2 cups frozen edamame beans, thawed
- 1 tablespoon olive oil
- 1/2 teaspoon sea salt
- 1/2 teaspoon chili flakes

Directions:

1. Before commencing the baking process, ensure that the oven has been preheated to 400°F (200°C).
2. In a bowl, toss the thawed edamame beans with olive oil, sea salt, and chili flakes until well coated.
3. Arrange the edamame beans in a single layer on a baking sheet.
4. Bake in the oven that has been preheated for 15-20 minutes, or until the beans achieve a slightly crispy, golden brown texture.
5. After taking them out of the oven, allow them to cool for a few minutes.
6. Serve the roasted edamame beans as a snack or appetizer.

Nutritional breakdown per serving:

Calories: 120 kcal, Protein: 10 grams, Carbohydrates: 10 grams, Fat: 5 grams, Saturated Fat: 0.5 grams, Cholesterol: 0 milligrams, Sodium: 300 milligrams, Fiber: 6 grams, and Sugar: 1 grams.

VEGAN BUFFALO CAULIFLOWER BITES WITH RANCH DIP

- Total Cooking Time: 40 minutes
- Prep Time: 15 minutes
- Servings: 4

Ingredients:

For the Buffalo Cauliflower Bites:

- 1 large head of cauliflower, cut into florets
- 1 cup all-purpose flour
- 1 cup plant-based milk
- 1 teaspoon garlic powder
- 1 teaspoon onion powder
- 1/2 teaspoon smoked paprika
- 1/2 teaspoon salt
- 1/4 teaspoon black pepper
- 1/2 cup hot sauce (e.g., Frank's RedHot or your favorite brand)
- 2 tablespoons melted vegan butter

For the Ranch Dip:

- 1 cup dairy-free yogurt (such as coconut or almond yogurt)
- 1 tablespoon lemon juice
- 1 teaspoon dried dill
- 1 teaspoon dried parsley
- 1/2 teaspoon garlic powder
- 1/2 teaspoon onion powder
- Salt and pepper, to taste

Directions:

For the Buffalo Cauliflower Bites:

1. Prepare for baking by heating the oven to 450°F (230°C) and placing parchment paper on a baking sheet for lining.
2. In a large bowl, whisk together the flour, plant-based milk, garlic powder, onion powder, smoked paprika, salt, and black pepper until smooth.

154

3. Cover each cauliflower floret with the batter, allowing any extra batter to drip off, and then arrange it on the prepared baking sheet.
4. Bake the cauliflower florets for 20-25 minutes, or until they are crispy and golden brown.
5. In a separate bowl, combine the hot sauce and melted vegan butter.
6. Take out the baked cauliflower from the oven and coat it evenly by tossing it in the hot sauce mixture.
7. Place the cauliflower back on the baking sheet with the coating and bake for an additional 5 minutes to allow the sauce to firm up.

For the Ranch Dip:

1. In a small bowl, combine the dairy-free yogurt, lemon juice, dried dill, dried parsley, garlic powder, onion powder, salt, and pepper. Mix well.
2. Adjust the seasoning to taste.

Serve the Vegan Buffalo Cauliflower Bites with the Ranch Dip.

Nutritional breakdown per serving:

Calories: 220 kcal, Protein: 8 grams, Carbohydrates: 35 grams, Fat: 6 grams, Saturated Fat: 1 grams, Cholesterol: 0 milligrams, Sodium: 1200 milligrams, Fiber: 6 grams, and Sugar: 6 grams.

VEGAN SPRING ROLLS WITH PEANUT DIPPING SAUCE

- Total Cooking Time: 30 minutes
- Prep Time: 20 minutes
- Servings: 4

Ingredients:

For the Spring Rolls:

- 8 rice paper wrappers
- 1 cup cooked rice noodles
- 1 cup shredded lettuce
- 1 cup julienned carrots
- 1 cup julienned cucumber
- 1/2 cup fresh mint leaves
- 1/2 cup fresh cilantro leaves
- 1/2 cup chopped roasted peanuts

For the Peanut Dipping Sauce:

- 1/4 cup peanut butter
- 2 tablespoons soy sauce
- 1 tablespoon maple syrup
- 1 tablespoon rice vinegar
- 1 clove garlic, minced
- 1/2 teaspoon grated ginger
- 2-3 tablespoons water (as needed for desired consistency)

Directions:

For the Peanut Dipping Sauce:

1. In a small bowl, whisk together the peanut butter, soy sauce, maple syrup, rice vinegar, minced garlic, and grated ginger.
2. Add water, one tablespoon at a time, until the sauce reaches your desired consistency. Set aside.

For the Spring Rolls:

1. Prepare a shallow dish with warm water.
2. Submerge a single rice paper wrapper into warm water for a few seconds until it becomes pliable.
3. Place the softened rice paper wrapper on a clean surface.
4. In the center of the wrapper, layer a small amount of rice noodles, shredded lettuce, julienned carrots, julienned cucumber, mint leaves, cilantro leaves, and chopped roasted peanuts.
5. Gently fold the sides of the wrapper over the filling, then tightly roll it from bottom to top, sealing the edges securely.
6. Submerge the remaining rice paper wrappers in warm water and fill them with the remaining ingredients, repeating the process.
7. Serve the spring rolls accompanied by the peanut dipping sauce.

Nutritional breakdown per serving:

Calories: 250 kcal, Protein: 8 grams, Carbohydrates: 35 grams, Fat: 10 grams, Saturated Fat: 2 grams, Cholesterol: 0 milligrams, Sodium: 400 milligrams, Fiber: 5 grams, and Sugar: 6 grams.

MINI VEGAN PIZZA BITES WITH WHOLE WHEAT DOUGH AND VEGGIE TOPPINGS

- Total Cooking Time: 30 minutes
- Prep Time: 15 minutes
- Servings: 4

Ingredients:

For the Whole Wheat Dough:

- 2 cups whole wheat flour
- 1 teaspoon active dry yeast
- 1 teaspoon sugar
- 1/2 teaspoon salt
- 3/4 cup warm water

For the Pizza Toppings:

- 1/2 cup tomato sauce or marinara sauce
- 1 cup vegan cheese, shredded
- 1/2 cup sliced bell peppers
- 1/2 cup sliced black olives
- 1/4 cup sliced red onions
- 1/4 cup chopped fresh basil leaves

Directions:

For the Whole Wheat Dough:

1. In a small bowl, combine the warm water, sugar, and active dry yeast. Let it sit for 5 minutes until the yeast becomes frothy.
2. Blend the whole wheat flour and salt in a sizable mixing bowl.
3. Blend the yeast mixture with the flour mixture and stir until the formation of a dough.
4. Work the dough on a surface lightly dusted with flour for around 5 minutes until it attains a smooth and elastic consistency.
5. Place the dough in a bowl that has been lightly coated with oil, then cover it with a fresh kitchen towel. Allow the dough to remain in a warm environment for approximately 1 hour, or until it has doubled in size.

<u>For the Pizza Bites:</u>

1. Before you begin, heat the oven to 425°F (220°C) and prepare a baking sheet by lining it with parchment paper.
2. After the dough has finished rising, delicately deflate it and divide it into small portions. Then, flatten each portion into a circular or square shape, ensuring it's approximately 1/4 inch thick.
3. Place the dough circles or squares on the prepared baking sheet.
4. Evenly distribute a light coating of tomato sauce or marinara sauce on each piece of dough.
5. Sprinkle vegan cheese on top of the sauce, followed by bell peppers, black olives, red onions, and fresh basil.
6. Put it in the oven that has been preheated and bake for 12-15 minutes, or until the crust turns a golden brown and the cheese has completely melted.
7. Once removed from the oven, let them cool for a few minutes prior to serving.

Nutritional breakdown per serving:

Calories: 250 kcal, Protein: 10 grams, Carbohydrates: 40 grams, Fat: 6 grams, Saturated Fat: 1 grams, Cholesterol: 0 milligrams, Sodium: 400 milligrams, Fiber: 8 grams, and Sugar: 2 grams.

BAKED KALE CHIPS WITH NUTRITIONAL YEAST

- Total Cooking Time: 25 minutes
- Prep Time: 10 minutes
- Servings: 4

Ingredients:

- 1 bunch kale
- 1 tablespoon olive oil
- 2 tablespoons nutritional yeast
- 1/2 teaspoon garlic powder
- 1/2 teaspoon onion powder
- 1/4 teaspoon salt
- 1/4 teaspoon black pepper

Directions:

1. Prior to commencing, it's crucial to verify that the oven has been preheated to 350°F (175°C) and that the baking sheet has been lined with parchment paper.
2. Cleanse the kale leaves meticulously and then gently dry them by patting.
3. After detaching the robust stems from the kale leaves, proceed to tear the leaves into bite-sized pieces.
4. In a large bowl, combine the torn kale leaves, olive oil, nutritional yeast, garlic powder, onion powder, salt, and black pepper. Combine until the kale leaves are uniformly covered.
5. Arrange the kale leaves in a uniform layer on the baking sheet that has been prepared.
6. You can cook in the oven until the kale leaves are crispy and lightly browned, which should take around 12-15 minutes.
7. After taking them out of the oven, allow the items to cool for a few minutes before serving.

Nutritional breakdown per serving:

Calories: 60 kcal, Protein: 4 grams, Carbohydrates: 7 grams, Fat: 3 grams, Saturated Fat: 0 grams, Cholesterol: 0 milligrams, Sodium: 150 milligrams, Fiber: 2 grams, and Sugar: 1 grams.

STUFFED MUSHROOMS WITH QUINOA AND SPINACH

- Total Cooking Time: 40 minutes
- Prep Time: 20 minutes
- Servings: 4

Ingredients:

- 16 large mushrooms
- 1 cup cooked quinoa
- 1 cup fresh spinach, chopped
- 1/2 cup diced tomatoes
- 1/4 cup diced red onion
- 2 cloves garlic, minced
- 2 tablespoons nutritional yeast
- 1 tablespoon olive oil
- 1/2 teaspoon dried oregano
- 1/2 teaspoon dried basil
- Salt and pepper, to taste

Directions:

- Prior to commencing, it's crucial to verify that the oven has been preheated to 350°F (175°C) and that the baking sheet has been lined with parchment paper.
- After removing the stems from the mushrooms, set them aside and then position the mushroom caps on the baking sheet that has been prepared.
- In a skillet placed over medium heat, warm the olive oil prior to adding the chopped red onion and minced garlic. Stir and cook until the onion becomes see-through.
- Add the chopped mushroom stems, diced tomatoes, and chopped spinach to the skillet. Cook for 3-4 minutes, or until the spinach wilts.
- Stir in the cooked quinoa, nutritional yeast, dried oregano, dried basil, salt, and pepper. Allow the flavors to blend by cooking for an extra 2-3 minutes.
- Spoon the quinoa and spinach mixture into each mushroom cap, filling them generously.
- Place the item in the preheated oven and cook for 15-20 minutes, or until the mushrooms reach desired tenderness and the filling is thoroughly heated.
- Kindly remove the items from the oven and let them cool for a short while before serving.

Nutritional breakdown per serving:

Calories: 120 kcal, Protein: 6 grams, Carbohydrates: 18 grams, Fat: 4 grams, Saturated Fat: 0.5 grams, Cholesterol: 0 milligrams, Sodium: 150 milligrams, Fiber: 4 grams, and Sugar: 3 grams.

SALSA AND BLACK BEAN STUFFED SWEET PEPPERS

- Total Cooking Time: 35 minutes
- Prep Time: 15 minutes
- Servings: 4

Ingredients:

- 8 sweet peppers (such as bell peppers), halved and seeds removed
- 1 cup cooked black beans
- 1 cup diced tomatoes
- 1/2 cup diced red onion
- 1/2 cup corn kernels
- 1/4 cup chopped fresh cilantro
- 1 tablespoon lime juice
- 1 teaspoon ground cumin
- 1/2 teaspoon chili powder
- Salt and pepper, to taste

Directions:

1. Begin the process by preheating the oven to 375°F (190°C) and placing parchment paper on a baking sheet.
2. In a large bowl, combine the black beans, diced tomatoes, diced red onion, corn kernels, chopped cilantro, lime juice, ground cumin, chili powder, salt, and pepper. Mix well.
3. Fill each halved sweet pepper with the black bean mixture, pressing it down gently.
4. Place the stuffed sweet peppers on the prepared baking sheet.
5. Cook in the oven that has been preheated for 20-25 minutes, or until the peppers are soft and have a slight char.
6. After removing from the oven, let them cool for a few minutes before serving.

Nutritional breakdown per serving:

Calories: 120 kcal, Protein: 6 grams, Carbohydrates: 26 grams, Fat: 1 grams, Saturated Fat: 0 grams, Cholesterol: 0 milligrams, Sodium: 150 milligrams, Fiber: 7 grams, and Sugar: 7 grams.

BEETROOT AND LENTIL HUMMUS WITH PITA BREAD

- Total Cooking Time: 40 minutes
- Prep Time: 15 minutes
- Servings: 4

Ingredients:

- 2 medium-sized beetroots, peeled and chopped
- 1 cup cooked lentils
- 3 tablespoons tahini
- 2 cloves garlic, minced
- 2 tablespoons lemon juice
- 1 tablespoon olive oil
- 1/2 teaspoon ground cumin
- Salt and pepper, to taste
- Pita bread, for serving

Directions:

1. Boil the chopped beetroots in a pot of boiling water until they are tender, usually for about 15-20 minutes. Afterward, drain the beetroots and let them cool down.
2. In a food processor, combine the cooked beetroots, cooked lentils, tahini, minced garlic, lemon juice, olive oil, ground cumin, salt, and pepper. Process until smooth and well combined.
3. Sample the hummus and make any necessary adjustments to the seasonings.
4. Transfer the beetroot and lentil hummus to a serving bowl.
5. Serve with pita bread or your choice of bread.

Nutritional breakdown per serving:

Calories: 180 kcal, Protein: 8 grams, Carbohydrates: 25 grams, Fat: 6 grams, Saturated Fat: 1 grams, Cholesterol: 0 milligrams, Sodium: 150 milligrams, Fiber: 7 grams, and Sugar: 5 grams.

CINNAMON APPLE CHIPS

- Total Cooking Time: 3 hours
- Prep Time: 15 minutes
- Servings: 4

Ingredients:

- 4 apples (preferably firm and crisp varieties like Granny Smith or Honeycrisp)
- 1 tablespoon cinnamon
- 1 tablespoon sugar (optional)

Directions:

1. Before using, set the oven to 200°F (95°C) and prepare two baking sheets by covering them with parchment paper.
2. Wash and core the apples. Slice the apples thinly into rounds, approximately 1/8 inch thick, and ensure to remove any seeds.
3. Blend the cinnamon and sugar (if desired) in a small bowl.
4. Please position the apple slices in an even layer on the baking sheets that have been prepared. Sprinkle the cinnamon mixture evenly over the apple slices.
5. Position the baking sheets in the preheated oven and bake for 2-3 hours, or until the apple slices achieve a crispy and dry texture. Remember to rotate the slices halfway through the baking time to ensure even drying.
6. Take out of the oven and allow the apple chips to cool down entirely before serving.

Nutritional breakdown per serving:

Calories: 60 kcal, Protein: 0 grams, Carbohydrates: 16 grams, Fat: 0 grams, Saturated Fat: 0 grams, Cholesterol: 0 milligrams, Sodium: 0 milligrams, Fiber: 3 grams, and Sugar: 11 grams.

ZUCCHINI AND CORN FRITTERS WITH SPICY CHIPOTLE MAYO

- Total Cooking Time: 30 minutes
- Prep Time: 15 minutes
- Servings: 4

Ingredients:

For the Fritters:

- 2 medium zucchinis, grated
- 1 cup corn kernels (fresh or frozen)
- 1/2 cup chickpea flour
- 1/4 cup nutritional yeast
- 2 green onions, finely chopped
- 2 tablespoons chopped fresh parsley
- 1 teaspoon ground cumin
- 1/2 teaspoon garlic powder
- Salt and pepper, to taste
- Olive oil, for frying

For the Spicy Chipotle Mayo:

- 1/2 cup vegan mayonnaise
- 1 tablespoon lime juice
- 1 teaspoon chipotle hot sauce (adjust to taste)
- Salt, to taste

Directions:

1. In a big bowl, mix grated zucchinis, corn kernels, chickpea flour, nutritional yeast, green onions, parsley, cumin, garlic powder, salt, and pepper. Stir thoroughly until everything is evenly mixed.
2. Heat a modest quantity of olive oil in a sizable skillet over medium heat.
3. Take a heaping tablespoon of the fritter mixture and shape it into a small patty. Place it in the skillet and flatten it slightly with a spatula. Repeat with the remaining mixture, making sure not to overcrowd the skillet.

4. Cook the fritters for about 3-4 minutes on each side, or until they are golden brown and crispy. You might have to cook them in multiple rounds, depending on the capacity of your skillet.
5. While the fritters are cooking, prepare the spicy chipotle mayo by combining the vegan mayonnaise, lime juice, chipotle hot sauce, and salt in a small bowl. Mix well.
6. Once the fritter preparation is complete, transfer them to a paper towel-lined plate to aid in absorbing any remaining oil.
7. Serve the zucchini and corn fritters warm with a side of spicy chipotle mayo for dipping.

Nutritional breakdown per serving:

Calories: 220 kcal, Protein: 8 grams, Carbohydrates: 27 grams, Fat: 10 grams, Saturated Fat: 1 grams, Cholesterol: 0 milligrams, Sodium: 300 milligrams, Fiber: 5 grams, and Sugar: 5 grams.

MINI QUICHES WITH TOFU AND VEGETABLE FILLINGS

- Total Cooking Time: 45 minutes
- Prep Time: 20 minutes
- Servings: 4

Ingredients:

For the Quiche Crust:

- 1 1/2 cups all-purpose flour
- 1/2 teaspoon salt
- 1/2 cup vegan butter, chilled and cubed
- 3-4 tablespoons ice water

For the Tofu and Vegetable Fillings:

- 1 block (14 ounces) firm tofu, drained and crumbled
- 1/2 cup diced bell peppers
- 1/2 cup diced zucchini
- 1/4 cup diced red onion
- 2 cloves garlic, minced
- 2 tablespoons nutritional yeast
- 1 tablespoon olive oil
- 1/2 teaspoon turmeric
- 1/2 teaspoon dried thyme
- Salt and pepper, to taste

Directions:

1. Turn the oven dial to 375°F (190°C) and wait until it reaches the specified temperature.
2. Mix together the all-purpose flour and salt in a large bowl to form the foundation of the quiche crust. Next, use a pastry cutter or your fingertips to blend in the chilled vegan butter until the mixture achieves a coarse, crumbly texture.
3. Slowly incorporate the ice water, adding one tablespoon at a time, and blend until the dough forms a cohesive mixture. Take care not to overmix. Shape the dough into a ball, then encase it in plastic wrap and place it in the refrigerator for 15 minutes.

4. In the meantime, prepare the tofu and vegetable fillings. In a skillet, heat the olive oil over medium heat. Add the diced bell peppers, zucchini, red onion, and minced garlic. Sauté until the vegetables are tender.
5. Combine the crumbled tofu, nutritional yeast, turmeric, dried thyme, salt, and pepper in the skillet. Stir thoroughly and cook for an extra 2-3 minutes. Then, remove from the heat.
6. To prepare, gently spread the refrigerated dough on a surface dusted with flour until it is approximately 1/8 inch thick. Following that, utilize a round cookie cutter or a glass to create circles that are suitable for fitting into the cups of a muffin tin.
7. Gently press each dough circle into the muffin tin cups to create mini quiche crusts.
8. Spoon the tofu and vegetable filling into each quiche crust, filling them about 3/4 full.
9. You have the option to place the quiches in the preheated oven and bake them for 20-25 minutes, or until they develop a golden brown hue and firm texture.
10. Upon removal from the oven, allow the quiches to cool for a few minutes before serving.

Nutritional breakdown per serving:

Calories: 320 kcal, Protein: 12 grams, Carbohydrates: 28 grams, Fat: 18 grams, Saturated Fat: 6 grams, Cholesterol: 0 milligrams, Sodium: 420 milligrams, Fiber: 4 grams, and Sugar: 2 grams.

CHOCOLATE AVOCADO MOUSSE CUPS

- Total Cooking Time: 15 minutes
- Prep Time: 10 minutes
- Servings: 4

Ingredients:

- 2 ripe avocados
- 1/4 cup unsweetened cocoa powder
- 1/4 cup of either maple syrup or agave nectar
- 1/4 cup almond milk
- 1 teaspoon vanilla extract
- Pinch of salt
- Fresh berries, for garnish (optional)
- Shredded coconut, for garnish (optional)
- Mint leaves, for garnish (optional)

Directions:

1. Blend ripe avocados, cocoa powder, maple syrup or agave nectar, almond milk, vanilla extract, and salt in a food processor or blender until the mixture is smooth and creamy.
2. Sample the mixture and modify the sweetness or cocoa flavor to your preference.
3. Transfer the chocolate avocado mousse to serving cups or glasses.
4. Chill the mousse for a minimum of 1 hour to enable it to set.
5. Before serving, garnish with fresh berries, shredded coconut, and mint leaves if desired.

Nutritional breakdown per serving:

Calories: 180 kcal, Protein: 3 grams, Carbohydrates: 19 grams, Fat: 12 grams, Saturated Fat: 2 grams, Cholesterol: 0 milligrams, Sodium: 10 milligrams, Fiber: 7 grams, and Sugar: 9 grams.

CONCLUSION

As we conclude this Mediterranean Diet Meal Prep Cookbook, it's evident that the Mediterranean diet offers a wealth of health benefits and a delicious approach to eating. The recipes and meal plans presented in this cookbook have highlighted the key principles of the Mediterranean diet, emphasizing the consumption of fruits, vegetables, whole grains, healthy fats, and lean proteins.

The historical and cultural significance of the Mediterranean diet has been underscored, showcasing the influence of various cultures and the traditions that have shaped the dietary patterns of countries bordering the Mediterranean Sea. The emphasis on fresh, seasonal ingredients and the avoidance of processed foods and refined carbohydrates align with the core principles of this dietary approach.

Research has consistently shown that adhering to a Mediterranean-style diet can help reduce the risk of cardiovascular diseases, manage weight, and promote overall well-being. The combination of foods in the Mediterranean diet appears to be protective against various diseases, making it a compelling and sustainable dietary pattern.

In conclusion, the Mediterranean Diet Meal Prep Cookbook has provided a comprehensive guide to embracing the Mediterranean diet as a balanced, non-restrictive eating plan that not only supports healthy aging and disease prevention but also acknowledges the value of social connection and bonding through communal dining experiences. We hope that the recipes and meal plans in this cookbook have inspired you to adopt a whole-diet approach and have equipped you with the tools to enjoy the health benefits and culinary delights of the Mediterranean diet. Here's to your health and enjoyment of the Mediterranean way of eating!

Printed in Great Britain
by Amazon

41820072R00099